GOURMET
GETAWAYS

GOURMET GETAWAYS

GETAWAYS

A Taste of North America's Top Resorts

BY PARIS PERMENTER & JOHN BIGLEY

Callawind
Publications Inc.

Gourmet Getaways: A Taste of North America's Top Resorts

CATALOGUING IN PUBLICATION DATA
Permenter, Paris
    Gourmet getaways : a taste of North America's top
resorts

Includes index.
ISBN 1-896511-07-4

    1. Cookery, Canadian. 2. Cookery, American.
3. Cookery, Mexican. 4. Cookery, Caribbean.
5. Resorts—North America. I. Bigley, John. II. Title.

TX907.P474 1997   641.5'097   C97-900622-8

Front and back cover design by Shari Blaukopf. Book design by Marcy Claman.
Copy editing by Jane Broderick. Photoediting by Shari Blaukopf. Indexing by Christine Jacobs.
Recipe consulting by Michael Greenfield.
Front cover photo of Grilled Salmon with Wild Rice Croquettes and Red Pepper Coulis (at Marriott's Bay Point Resort Village, Panama City Beach, Florida) by Robert Overton.

10 9 8 7 6 5 4 3 2 1

Printed in Canada.
All product/brand names are trademarks or registered trademarks of their respective trademark holders. Resort information and prices in this book are subject to change without notice.

Callawind Publications Inc.
3383 Sources Boulevard, Suite 205, Dollard-des-Ormeaux, Quebec H9B 1Z8 Canada
2083 Hempstead Turnpike, Suite 355, East Meadow, New York 11554-1730 USA
http://www.callawind.com   e-mail: info@callawind.com

Acknowledgments

. . . .

In researching this guide, we quickly learned that North America is home to many types of resorts. Their geography may make the beach resorts seem a far cry from the mountain getaways, but the message remains the same: welcome home.

We found that whether golf, tennis, beach, or mountain, these resorts welcomed visitors with friendly staff, fascinating activities, and flavorful food. We would like to thank all the resort personnel who made our stays so wonderful, from the desk clerks and bellmen who gave us our first introduction to the resort, to the restaurant staff and chefs who made our meals so memorable, to the maids and housekeeping staff who made our stays so comfortable.

We would also like to thank those who helped on the home front during our many research trips. Our gratitude goes to our friends Laurie and Tim Kibel, Cliff and Clara Trahan, Sam Bertron, and Rebecca Lowe for their assistance during our travels. As always, special thanks go to Mom and Dad, Carlene and Richard Permenter, for all their help when we had to hit the road.

Thanks are also in order to our daughter, Lauren Bigley, who not only traveled with us on many research trips but also tested recipes and fact-checked the manuscript.

Collecting and fact-checking the recipes and details of the resorts was facilitated by many public relations agencies across the continent. Their cooperation made our job much easier.

CONTENTS

....

INTRODUCTION

. . . .

From powder-white alpine slopes to powder-white tropical beaches, North American resorts offer travelers a place to sample tasty and exotic morsels, make new friends, renew old loves, learn new sports, and simply unwind.

Whether your idea of a vacation is feasting on culinary delights, shushing down the slopes, hitting the greens, perfecting your backhand, indulging in spa treatments, or relaxing under a towering palm tree, you'll find North America has just the getaway for you.

Selection of the resorts on these pages was no simple task. Throughout North America, we found lavish resorts that offer the utmost in plush accommodations, attentive service, and wonderful dining. Ultimately, we decided to include our favorites — resorts, in every price range, for a diverse clientele. Some are designed for adults only, while many welcome families and offer a variety of supervised children's programs. Some feature rustic accommodations, with a blurring of the line between indoors and out, while others have suites fit for a king.

But they all have two common features. First, every resort included here is just that — a resort; while North America is dotted with top-of-the-line hotels, we selected only those locations where vacationers could, if they chose to, never leave the premises for their entire stay. Second, every resort in this guide is noted for its superb dining opportunities, making it a true gourmet getaway.

Whether you use this book as a cookbook in bringing to your home kitchen a taste of your last vacation, as a guide in selecting your next vacation, or as an opportunity to do some armchair traveling and feasting, we hope it conveys to you some measure of the joy we experienced in visiting these resorts. Whether you eventually savor the dishes in an exotic resort environment or in your own dining room, we say: bon appetit, salud, enjoy.

Using this Guide

Resort prices vary greatly with the season and type of accommodation. The dollar signs (US$) that follow the telephone number(s) of each resort indicate the price range of a standard room for two adults for one night during high season.

$: under $201
$$: $201 – $300
$$$: $301 – $400
$$$$: over $400

CANADA

Yukon
Territory

Northwest Territories

Victoria
Island

Baffin
Island

British
Columbia

Alberta

Saskatchewan

Manitoba

Newfoundland

Tofino

Whistler
Vancouver
Malahat
Victoria

Jasper

Edmonton

Lake
Louise
Yoho
National
Park

Calgary
Banff

Québec

Ontario

New
Brunswick

P.E.I.

Mont
Tremblant

Québec

Montréal

Huntsville
Ottawa

Toronto

St. Andrews-
By-the-Sea

Nova Scotia

Saint John

OPPOSITE: *For more
than a century
vacationers have
reveled in the scenic
beauty of Château
Lake Louise in Alberta.*

Canada 11

Banff Springs Hotel

*T*he Banff Springs Hotel has long been renowned for its spectacular setting in the Canadian Rockies. Now it is earning accolades for its magnificent spa, Solace.

Banff, Alberta

(800) 441-1414

$$

mountain / spa

Here, guests are pampered in an environment every bit as notable as the one beyond its walls in the great outdoors. Enough luxurious treatments are offered to keep any discerning vacationer purring with contentment.

At this resort, the spa tradition dates back to the turn of the century. In the early 1900s, Banff's invigorating pools and therapeutic body treatments were much sought after. Today, with the addition of the $12-million spa, the hotel is once again a place to "take the waters." At this European-style spa, guests are greeted with cascading waterfalls, open fireplaces, solariums, 16 private treatment rooms, steam rooms, and saunas. Treatments range from massages to mineral baths to facials.

Beauty surrounds you everywhere at this castle in the Rockies. Materials were imported from around the globe to build the hotel. Styled after the baronial castles of Scotland, the hotel took 18 years to construct.

Although the resort offers many dining options, an increasingly popular one is the spa menu at Solace, which features low-fat, low-calorie cuisine. Diners begin with appetizers such as 45-calorie avocado terrine (see recipe opposite) or 86-calorie chilled-fruit soup, then move on to healthful entrées like fillet of trout poached with a selection of vegetables in a saffron broth or spelt and buckwheat crêpes with assorted mushrooms.

ABOVE: *The Grapes Wine Bar is one of many eateries that exude elegance and provide attentive service at this resort.*

AT A GLANCE: *770 rooms, some with mountain view. 17 restaurants, cooking courses, fitness center, spa, steam room, sauna, whirlpool, beauty salon, shops, movie theaters, indoor/outdoor (heated) pool, tennis, golf, bicycling, cross-country skiing, skating, snowshoeing, dogsledding.* NEARBY: *supervised children's programs, rollerblading, hiking, nature walking, horseback riding, river rafting, fishing, downhill skiing, snowboarding, snowmobiling, sleigh rides.*

Avocado Terrine with Salsa Vinaigrette

Avocado Terrine:

Spinach or Swiss chard to line mold

1¾ ounces spinach

9 ounces avocado, pitted and peeled

1½ tablespoons lemon juice

¾ cup low-fat yogurt

Salt and pepper to taste

Tabasco to taste

3½ tablespoons mineral water

½ tablespoon gelatin

Salsa Vinaigrette (yields about 2 cups):

1 cup diced, seeded tomatoes

⅓ cup chopped green, yellow, and red bell peppers

¼ cup chopped onion

1½ tablespoons chopped herbs (such as chives, parsley, and basil)

1 small piece jalapeño, seeded and chopped

¼ cup aged balsamic vinegar

1 teaspoon olive oil

1 tablespoon salt

1 tablespoon pepper

Prepare the terrine. Blanch the spinach or Swiss chard and use it to line a mold.

Blanch the 1¾ ounces spinach, then dip it in ice water and dry well. Purée. Purée the avocado with the lemon juice, then blend it with the spinach purée and the yogurt. Season with the salt and pepper and Tabasco. Stir in the mineral water. Fold in the gelatin. Quickly turn the mixture into the lined mold and allow to set for 8 hours or refrigerate overnight.

Prepare the vinaigrette. Mix all the ingredients.

Yield: 14 appetizer servings

. . . .

BELOW: *Breathtaking beauty surrounds visitors everywhere at the Banff Springs Hotel.*

Buffalo Mountain Lodge

Tucked into a corner of Banff National Park, this charming hand-hewn log structure offers guests the opportunity to truly experience the Canadian Rockies.

Banff, Alberta

(800) 661-1367

$ – $$

mountain

Set amidst nine wooded acres of beautiful tall pines on a slope of Tunnel Mountain — which was once known as Sleeping Buffalo — this resort, which opened in 1988, offers seclusion and privacy. Buffalo Mountain Lodge also has two fully equipped conference facilities.

The lobby of the main lodge — the perfect setting for its cozy bar — features bent willow, cherry, and pine furniture, high, beamed ceilings, and a massive fieldstone fireplace with a magnificent buffalo head mounted above it.

Buffalo Mountain Lodge is often referred to as the birthplace of Rocky Mountain cuisine. Its menus, which use ingredients indigenous to the region, reflect the rich bounty of Western Canada: venison, elk, caribou, buffalo, trout, arctic char, and regional varieties of mushrooms, nuts, and herbs. Dining begins with dishes such as salmon pastrami served over cornmeal waffles with caper crème fraîche or venison phyllo rolls with acorn squash coulis. The main course might feature caribou ravioli with cilantro-basil pesto and goat cheese, potato lasagne with wild mushrooms and leeks over four-cheese sauce, rack of white-tailed deer with Pinot Noir sauce and stuffed artichoke hearts, or roasted free-range game hen with caramelized apples and onion broth.

This resort welcomes visitors year round. In the summer, guests take advantage of the many walking paths and hiking trails that lead from the lodge. Deer and elk can be seen roaming the grounds daily. In winter, vacationers ski the miles of cross-country trails. Buffalo Mountain Lodge is only a 20-minute walk from the center of Banff, and just a short drive from the world-famous downhill ski areas of Mount Norquay, Sunshine Village, and Lake Louise.

Above: *Set in Banff National Park, the Buffalo Mountain Lodge is often called the birthplace of Rocky Mountain cuisine.*

At a glance: *108 units with fireplace, some with private balcony/patio, mountain view. 2 restaurants, cooking courses, fitness center, sauna, hiking, nature walking.* Nearby: *spa, beauty salon, shops, movie theaters, indoor/outdoor (heated) pool, tennis, golf, bicycling, horseback riding, downhill/cross-country skiing, snowboarding, skating, snowshoeing, dogsledding, sleigh rides.*

Smoked Pepper Duck with Cheddar Cup and Cranberry Chutney

Cranberry Chutney (yields 2 cups):
1 cup sugar
½ cup orange juice
1 cup Merlot
1½ cups cranberries (frozen, thawed)
1 cup chopped rhubarb (frozen, thawed)
Zest of 1 orange
1 tablespoon chopped ginger
1 (2-inch) cinnamon stick
1 tablespoon cracked black pepper

Cheddar Cups:
½ cup coarsely grated sharp white Cheddar cheese

Vinaigrette:
6 – 8 fennel seeds
Zest and juice of 1 lemon
1 tablespoon black pepper
Salt to taste
Dash of raspberry vinegar
¼ cup olive oil
2 tablespoons chopped herbs (such as chives or flat-leaf parsley)

Duck:
2 (7-ounce) smoked pepper duck breasts (see note)

Assembly:
1 cup mixed winter greens

Prepare the chutney. Caramelize the sugar in a stainless steel saucepan over low heat, stirring constantly, until golden (do not let it burn). Add the orange juice and cook until blended. Stir in the remaining ingredients. Simmer for 30 minutes or until the mixture has the consistency of jam. Skim any foam from the surface and remove the cinnamon stick.

The chutney may be prepared up to a week in advance. Store in jars in the refrigerator. Bring to room temperature before serving.

Prepare the Cheddar cups. In a non-stick sauté pan over medium heat, sprinkle a thin layer of the cheese the size of a saucer (about 2 tablespoons). When it is bubbly and golden around the edges, remove the entire sheet of cheese with a plastic spatula and drape it over a juice glass. It will harden quickly. Once it is set, carefully remove the cheese cup. Make 3 more using the same method.

Prepare the vinaigrette. Roast the fennel seeds in a dry (unoiled) pan until they start to pop. Add the lemon zest and remove from heat. When slightly cooled, add the remaining ingredients.

Prepare the duck. Warm the duck for 5 – 6 minutes in a preheated 300°F oven.

To assemble, thinly slice the duck and arrange in a circular pattern on each plate. Place a Cheddar cup in the center of the plate and fill it with the mixed greens. Drizzle the vinaigrette over the greens and spoon the cranberry chutney over the duck. Serve immediately.

Note: Smoked pepper duck is available in specialty food shops. Smoked goose breast, also available in specialty food shops, can be used as a substitute.

Yield: 4 appetizer servings

ABOVE: *The fashionably rustic Buffalo Mountain Lodge offers seclusion and privacy.*

Rimrock Resort Hotel

With Canadian grande dames *Château Lake Louise* and the *Banff Springs Hotel* as neighbors, it isn't easy being the new kid on the Banff block.

Banff, Alberta

(800) 661-1587

$ – $$

mountain

But the Rimrock Resort Hotel has proven itself equal to the challenge, garnering such accolades as the coveted AAA Four Diamond rating (the only Banff hotel to do so).

Situated in Banff National Park, this resort takes advantage of its spectacular setting with windows offering panoramic views from every location, from the lobby to the guest rooms. Outdoors, vacationers quickly learn to always keep an eye out for elk and deer.

Perched on Sulphur Mountain, the resort is within walking distance of the Sulphur Mountain Gondola and the famous rejuvenating Sulphur Mountain Hot Pools.

This resort also features a full-service exercise facility. The Rimrock Health Club keeps guests on the move with stair-stepping machines, treadmills, weight-training equipment, and an indoor swimming pool.

As the day comes to a close, guests are likely to find themselves in Rimrock's sophisticated Ristorante Classico, which specializes in Northern Italian dishes, or the Primrose Restaurant, which features spinach fettuccine with chicken and wild mushrooms (see recipe opposite).

ABOVE: *This distinctive resort located near the hot pools in Banff National Park takes full advantage of its spectacular setting.*

AT A GLANCE: *324 rooms, some with mountain view; 21 suites with whirlpool, some with fireplace, private balcony, mountain view. 2 restaurants, fitness center, steam room, sauna, whirlpool, beauty salon, shops, indoor pool, bicycling, hiking, nature walking, skating.* NEARBY: *spa, movie theaters, outdoor pool, tennis, golf, horseback riding, fishing, hunting, downhill/cross-country skiing, snowboarding, snowshoeing, snowmobiling, dogsledding, sleigh rides.*

Spinach Fettuccine with Chicken and Wild Mushrooms

Béchamel Sauce (yields 4 cups):
¼ cup butter
¾ cup all-purpose flour
1 quart cold milk
Pinch of nutmeg
½ bay leaf
¼ teaspoon salt

Fettuccine:
1 pound boneless, skinless chicken
   breast, diced
½ cup mixed dried or fresh wild
   mushrooms (such as chanterelle,
   shiitake, oyster, white)
2½ tablespoons olive oil
1 teaspoon minced garlic
1 teaspoon minced shallot
¼ cup dry white wine
1 cup béchamel sauce
2 cups whipping cream
1¼ pounds fresh spinach fettuccine
   noodles
1 tablespoon chopped basil
Salt and pepper to taste
½ cup grated Parmesan cheese
4 – 6 basil leaves
Red, green, and yellow bell peppers,
   seeded and very finely diced

Prepare the béchamel sauce. Melt the butter in a saucepan. Mix in the flour. Cook for a few minutes, then add the milk gradually. Add the nutmeg, bay leaf, and salt and let simmer for at least 30 minutes. If the sauce becomes too thick, add more milk. Strain through a cheesecloth or strainer. Reserve 1 cup for this recipe and refrigerate the remainder for later use.

Prepare the fettuccine. In a hot pan, sauté the chicken and mushrooms in the oil until the chicken is almost cooked throughout. Add the garlic and shallot and sauté for 2 minutes. Deglaze with the wine and let the wine reduce until it is almost gone. Add the béchamel sauce and cream and reduce for 5 – 6 minutes or until slightly thickened.

Cook the noodles in boiling salted water for 6 minutes or until al dente. Combine the noodles with the chicken mixture. Add the basil and salt and pepper. Top with the cheese. Garnish with the basil leaves and diced bell pepper.

Yield: 4 – 6 servings

BELOW: *An active day at the Rimrock Resort Hotel concludes with a superb meal.*

Jasper Park Lodge

Winter or summer, Jasper Park Lodge recalls the most glamorous days of national parks, a time when the director of Canadian Pacific Railways reasoned, "If we can't export the scenery, we'll import the tourists," thus bringing to the wilderness both the railway and an era of grand hotels and rustic pleasures.

Jasper, Alberta

(800) 441-1414

$ – $$$

golf/mountain

The beauty and cachet of Jasper Park Lodge, which is set on a thousand acres of alpine terrain, have drawn many big names to its doorstep. Such celebrities as Marilyn Monroe, Jimmy Stewart, Pierre Trudeau, and Sir Arthur Conan Doyle have stayed at this mountain retreat, where elk have the right of way on the 18-hole championship golf course.

The elegance and eclecticism of the resort are equaled by its fine dining. The Edith Cavell Room, which is frequently cited as one of Canada's top restaurants, features the creations of executive chef David MacGillivray. "I enjoy preparing menus that are based on the heritage of good home cooking," says MacGillivray. "I also like using ingredients that are indigenous to Alberta, such as our grain-fed Alberta beef, Alberta pork, wild mushrooms, and grains." The wonderful dishes are served with vintage wines, and, as a bonus for diners, the Edith Cavell Room features a view of the majestic Rocky Mountains. Other dining choices at Jasper Park Lodge include the smartly casual Moose's Nook, which serves Canadian cuisine.

As well as rooms and suites, Jasper Park Lodge offers luxury cabins: the eight-bedroom Milligan Manor has four whirlpool tubs, a service kitchen, and a dining table that sits 14 people.

AT A GLANCE: *365 rooms, some with private patio; 68 suites, some with Jacuzzi, fireplace, private balcony/ patio, scenic view; 9 (2 – 8-bedroom) cabins, some with whirlpool. 7 restaurants, cooking courses, fitness center, spa, steam room, sauna, beauty salon, shops, supervised children's programs, outdoor (heated) pool, tennis, golf, bicycling, rollerblading, hiking, nature walking, horseback riding, beach, scuba diving, snorkeling, marina, river rafting, fishing, downhill/cross-country skiing, snowboarding, skating, snowshoeing, dogsledding, sleigh rides.* NEARBY: *movie theaters, indoor pool, indoor tennis, windsurfing, boating, snowmobiling.*

ABOVE: *Elk have the right of way on the rolling golf course.*

Walnut-Crusted Chicken Breasts with Rhubarb-Onion Chutney

The tart, crisp rhubarb of early spring lends a tang to this chutney, while the nutty-tasting breading keeps the chicken moist and tender.

Rhubarb-Onion Chutney (yields 3 cups):
1 large yellow onion, finely diced
4 cups diced fresh rhubarb
¼ cup white wine vinegar
¼ cup sugar
¼ cup raisins
2 tablespoons minced ginger
2 tablespoons minced garlic
2 tablespoons Madras curry powder
½ teaspoon salt
2 tablespoons chopped mint

Walnut-Crusted Chicken Breasts:
6 boneless, skinless chicken breasts, pounded ½-inch thick
Salt and pepper to taste
1 cup all-purpose flour
3 eggs
½ cup water
2 cups coarsely ground walnuts
½ cup vegetable oil
Sprigs of mint (optional)

Prepare the chutney. In a medium saucepan, combine all the ingredients except the mint and bring to a low boil over medium heat. Reduce heat and cook, stirring frequently, for 30 minutes or until the onions and rhubarb are tender and the chutney has thickened. Remove from heat and let cool, then add the mint. Place in three 1-cup sterilized canning jars and store in the refrigerator for up to 3 weeks or in the freezer for up to 2 months.

Prepare the chicken. Season with salt and pepper and dredge in the flour, shaking off the excess. Beat the eggs with the water until well combined. Dip the chicken in the egg mixture, then dredge in the walnuts, coating evenly.

Preheat the oven to 250° – 300°F. In a large, heavy sauté pan, heat half the oil over medium heat. Place three of the chicken breasts in the pan and cook for 5 – 7 minutes per side or until golden brown. Keep warm in the oven. Repeat the procedure for the three remaining breasts.

Serve with the rhubarb-onion chutney and garnish with the sprigs of mint, if desired.

Yield: 6 servings

BELOW: *Any season of the year Jasper Park Lodge brings to mind the glorious heydey of national parks.*

Château Lake Louise

*G*racing the shores of Lake Louise in Banff National Park, Château Lake Louise has long been a popular getaway for the world's notables: Prince Rainier, King Edward VIII, Cary Grant, Bing Crosby, Alfred Hitchcock, Gene Autry. The list goes on.

Lake Louise,
Alberta

(800) 441-1414

$$

mountain

Château Lake Louise was designed as "a hotel for the outdoor adventurer and alpinist," in the words of railroad tycoon Cornelius Van Horne when Canadian Pacific Railways was about to embark on the great venture of bringing tourism to the Canadian Rockies. Van Horne's dream was realized when the magnificent hotel opened on the shores of Lake Louise in the shadow of Victoria Glacier.

Today, more than a century later, the resort has more to offer than ever, following a complete restoration of its guest rooms. Vacationers can enjoy a full day of activities any season of the year. Winter offers the promise of full days on the slopes in this, the largest ski area in Canada. In summer, guests favor long walks in the clear alpine air.

Whatever the season, evenings are for fine dining, and the choices are wide. The Poppy Room Family Restaurant, with a unique Bavarian atmosphere, overlooks the gardens and Lake Louise. The Tom Wilson Dining Room is known for its Continental menu. The Victoria Dining Room, now restored to its 1913 grandeur, tempts visitors to dine and dance surrounded by wood paneling and hand-painted motifs. The Edelweiss Dining Room offers European cuisine featuring many game dishes served against a backdrop of romantic Lake Louise.

ABOVE: *Eight restaurants present a variety of dining options.*

AT A GLANCE: *428 rooms and 69 suites, all with whirlpool, private balcony, mountain/lake view. 8 restaurants, fitness center, steam room, whirlpool, beauty salon, shops, supervised children's programs, indoor pool, bicycling, hiking, nature walking, horseback riding, canoeing, cross-country skiing, skating, snowshoeing, ice climbing, sleigh rides.* NEARBY: *spa, movie theaters, tennis, golf, river rafting, fishing, downhill skiing, snowboarding, snowmobiling, dogsledding.*

Pouding Chômeur

This hearty dessert is a traditional French Canadian dish.

2 teaspoons plus 1¼ cups all-purpose
    flour
1 cup brown sugar
2 cups water
1 cup maple syrup
1 tablespoon butter
2 eggs
1 cup granulated sugar
¼ teaspoon vanilla
¼ cup vegetable shortening
2 teaspoons baking powder
¼ teaspoon salt
¾ cup milk

Preheat the oven to 350°F. Grease a 12 x 8 x 2-inch baking dish.

Mix the 2 teaspoons of flour into the brown sugar, then place in a saucepan with the water, maple syrup, and butter. Bring to a boil, then remove from heat and set aside.

Whip the eggs, granulated sugar, and vanilla. Add the shortening and mix.

Sift the 1¼ cups flour, baking powder, and salt. Add this to the egg mixture alternately with the milk.

Turn the batter into the prepared baking dish. Slowly pour the cooked liquid mixture over the batter. Bake for 35 – 40 minutes or until the top is golden brown and the center is firm when the pan is shaken. Let stand for 10 minutes, then serve warm.

Yield: 6 – 10 servings

. . . .
BELOW: *Since 1890, guests have been flocking to Château Lake Louise for its spectacular vistas.*

Deer Lodge

T his lodge, which has been welcoming visitors to one of Canada's most scenic regions since 1921, offers rustic charm to vacationers eager to get away and nestle in the Rocky Mountains.

Lake Louise, Alberta

(800) 661-1595

$

mountain

Deer Lodge has an interesting history. When Canadian Pacific Railways built its grand resorts, it also erected a series of day lodges as stopovers for hikers. Three additions to the Lake Louise hikers' lodge — a log teahouse, tucked behind Château Lake Louise, a drugstore, and a YWCA residence — would eventually become Deer Lodge.

The Mount Fairview Dining Room serves Rocky Mountain cuisine, game and other fresh ingredients prepared by chefs trained in classical French cooking using innovative California techniques. Appetizers include Rocky Mountain game platter, featuring smoked pepper duck breast, venison salametti, air-dried buffalo, game pâté, venison ham, mustard melon, and cranberry relish. Entrées include British Columbia salmon, rack of Alberta lamb in garlic, caribou medallions in a sun-dried cherry pepper sauce with wild-mushroom penne, and stuffed pork tenderloin. The restaurant features an extensive wine list.

Definitely the place for those who want to get away from it all, Deer Lodge is as tranquil and serene as its alpine surroundings. There are no televisions or telephones in the rooms, nor are there glitzy après-ski activities: evenings are spent star-gazing or enjoying the strains of peaceful music. Deer Lodge also features walks with the innkeeper and schedules lectures about the area surrounding Lake Louise. One superb amenity is a rooftop hot tub featuring a spectacular view of Victoria Glacier.

ABOVE: *This is a destination for those who value tranquility in an historic setting.*

AT A GLANCE: *73 rooms, some with mountain view. 2 restaurants, sauna, hiking, nature walking. NEARBY: fitness center, spa, beauty salon, shops, movie theaters, indoor / outdoor (heated) pool, tennis, golf, bicycling, horseback riding, downhill / cross-country skiing, snowboarding, skating, snowshoeing, dogsledding, sleigh rides.*

Venison Sirloin in Baco Noir Sauce

Brown Stock: (yields 12 cups):
5 pounds beef or veal bones
3 ounces tomato paste
½ pound carrots, unpeeled, cut into ½-inch pieces
½ pound celery, cut into ½-inch pieces
½ pound white onion, coarsely chopped
1 sprig of thyme
1 bay leaf
1 garlic bulb
6 black peppercorns
¼ cup dry red wine

Baco Noir Sauce:
¼ cup sugar
½ cup Baco Noir (Cabernet Sauvignon or Merlot may be substituted)
1 tablespoon balsamic vinegar
1 cup brown stock (see accompanying recipe, or use dark game stock from a specialty food shop)
1 sprig of rosemary
1 bay leaf
2 juniper berries
Salt and pepper to taste
½ cup dried cherries, presoaked

Venison:
2 tablespoons vegetable oil
6 garlic cloves, minced
1 tablespoon dried red chili flakes
1 tablespoon ground cinnamon
4 (8-ounce) venison loins (or substitute beef or pork tenderloin)
6 tablespoons toasted black and white peppercorns
Coarse salt

Prepare the stock. Preheat the oven to 400°F and roast the bones for 60 minutes. Coat with the tomato paste, add the carrot, celery, and onion and continue roasting until the paste is caramelized. Skim off the fat and turn the mixture into an 8-quart stock pot. Add the thyme, bay leaf, garlic, and peppercorns. Deglaze the roasting pan with the wine, then add the liquid to the stock pot. Top with cold water and simmer for 8 hours over low heat (do not boil). Strain through a cheesecloth and skim off the fat. Reserve 1 cup for this recipe and store the remainder (in the refrigerator for up to 4 days, in the freezer for up to 3 months).

Prepare the sauce. Caramelize the sugar in a stainless steel pot over low heat, stirring constantly (do not let it burn). Deglaze with the wine and vinegar and reduce by half. Add the stock, rosemary, bay leaf, and berries and reduce by half. Season. Strain and add the cherries. Keep warm.

Prepare the venison. Make a marinade using the oil, garlic, chili, and cinnamon and marinate in the refrigerator for 4 – 6 hours or overnight. Preheat the oven to 400°F. Pat the meat dry and roll it in the pepper and salt. Pan sear, then roast in the oven for 10 – 12 minutes. Let rest for 5 minutes before slicing.

Serve with the warm Baco Noir sauce.
Yield: 4 servings

BELOW: *The mood at Deer Lodge is as peaceful and serene as its pristine alpine surroundings.*

The Aerie

If The Aerie seems the stuff of **Lifestyles of the Rich and Famous,** *it's no wonder: Robin Leach has included this opulent resort on his television show. And it isn't hard to see why.*

*Malahat,
British Columbia*

(250) 743-7115

$

mountain

Built in the style of a Mediterranean villa, this resort features over-the-top luxury: Helicopter pad for vacationers on the run. Persian and Chinese silk carpets. Oversized whirlpools surrounded by gold-leaf columns. Fourteen-karat-gold dining room ceiling.

But the real gold at this resort is its setting. Guests of The Aerie are enveloped in the serene atmosphere of Vancouver Island and treated to views of the Olympic Mountains, the Gulf Islands, and tranquil inlets. Romantic, remote, and restful, this resort is for those looking for a true getaway.

The spa treatments at The Aerie are indulgent as well. The Aesthetically Yours spa offers massage, aromatherapy, lymph-draining facials, toning facials, and deep-cleansing facials. Beauty treatments such as waxing, manicure, pedicure, and make-up services are available.

Gourmet breakfast is standard fare. And to nourish the mind and the spirit, as well as the body, The Aerie even features a library and a chapel right on the premises.

Vacationers also find plenty of attractions in the surrounding area, such as golf, sailing, whale watching, hiking, and horseback riding.

After witnessing a dramatic Pacific sunset, guests dine on French cuisine with a West Coast flair. Chef Leo Schuster's menus reflect the seasons, featuring dishes such as medallions of venison with sun-dried cherry sauce, carpaccio of beef with caper, berry, and tomato relish, and pan-seared Pacific halibut with ragout of spring asparagus and morels.

ABOVE: *Set in the serene atmosphere of Vancouver Island, The Aerie is for those vacationers who crave a true getaway.*

AT A GLANCE: *10 rooms with scenic view, some with Jacuzzi, most with private balcony / patio; 13 suites with Jacuzzi, fireplace, private balcony / patio, scenic view. Restaurant, cooking courses (selective dates), spa, sauna, whirlpool, beauty salon, indoor pool, tennis.* NEARBY: *fitness center, movie theaters, golf, bicycling, hiking, nature walking, horseback riding, beach, watersports, boating, marina, fishing, whale watching, winery tours.*

Grilled Oysters with Sweet Peppers and Chive Butter

Oysters:
12 large fresh oysters, shucked
1 tablespoon lime juice
Black pepper to taste
1 red bell pepper, seeded and cut into
    ¾-inch triangles
1 yellow bell pepper, seeded and cut
    into ¾-inch triangles
2 tablespoons olive oil

Chive Butter:
1 tablespoon chopped shallot
Olive oil
¼ cup dry white wine
¼ cup fish stock
3 tablespoons butter
2 tablespoons snipped chives
Black pepper to taste

Garnish:
Chive blossoms

Prepare the oysters. In a bowl, gently mix the oysters, lime juice, and black pepper. Let stand in the refrigerator. In a separate bowl, mix the bell peppers, oil, and more black pepper. Let stand for several hours.

Prepare the chive butter. Sauté the shallot in olive oil over medium heat. Add the wine and fish stock and let the liquid reduce slightly. Whisk in the butter a tablespoon at a time and remove from heat (do not boil or the sauce will separate). Add the chives and pepper. Keep warm.

Place the oysters on a hot, well-oiled grill. Cook for 1 minute, then turn. Add the bell peppers and cook for 1 more minute. Remove from the grill and pat with paper towels to remove excess oil.

To serve, pour a small pool of the chive butter onto each plate. Place 3 oysters on each pool and alternate the red and yellow peppers between the oysters. Garnish with the chive blossoms.

Yield: 4 appetizer servings

• • • • • • • • •
ABOVE: *At The Aerie, fine dining is an ideal way to cap a day of golf, hiking, horseback riding, sailing, or whale watching.*

The Wickaninnish Inn

Perched on the western edge of the continent, where Vancouver Island meets the Pacific Ocean, this inn provides a haven in a storm.

Tofino,
British Columbia

(800) 333-4604

$ – $$

beach / fishing

Literally. During the months of November through February, The Wickaninnish Inn sells a special "winter storm" getaway, offering guests a unique opportunity to experience the drama of coastal gales, with impressive waves rolling over the adjacent mile-and-a-half-long beach. At other times of the year the inn provides a more peaceful shelter. It fulfills the promise of a stress-free vacation, with whale watching, reflective beach walks, ocean kayaking, and diverse marine excursions.

Situated on Chesterman Beach, on the unspoiled west coast of Vancouver Island, the current Wickaninnish Inn is a reincarnation of a more rustic one. The original inn, located on Long Beach, was converted to a marine interpretive center following the creation of the Pacific Rim National Park Reserve a quarter of a century ago. Building an inn that would embrace the same spirit and feature a similar style was the idea of Dr. Howard McDiarmid and his family. The inn is a true family operation: all three of McDiarmid's sons are engaged in its management.

The Wickaninnish Inn is surrounded by the sea, verdant forest forming a backdrop. In keeping with its commitment to nature, the resort's furniture — the work of master carver Henry Nolla — is fashioned from recycled old-growth fir, western red cedar, and driftwood, while its guest rooms are fitted with wool sisal carpets and stone tiles. The rooms also feature oversized soaker tubs — many with their own view — along with fireplaces and balconies.

The Pointe Restaurant and On-the-Rocks Bar, which affords a magnificent 240-degree panorama of the pounding surf, highlights the creations of chef Rodney J. Butters. The restaurant serves West Coast cuisine featuring Vancouver Island seafood and vegetables and regionally produced wines.

Guests who bring their own equipment or rent it at a nearby facility can scuba dive, snorkel, surf, windsurf, or kayak on the Wickaninnish premises.

ABOVE: The Wickaninnish Inn offers a stress-free vacation on the shores of Vancouver Island.

AT A GLANCE: *46 rooms with fireplace, private balcony, beach / ocean view, some with whirlpool. Restaurant, nature walking, beach.* NEARBY: *beauty salon, shops, tennis, golf, bicycling, hiking, horseback riding, boating, marina, fishing, watersports equipment rental.*

Layered Yams

**4 large yams, peeled and cut into
⅓-inch slices**
1 yellow onion, cut into ⅓-inch slices
**3 tablespoons chopped lovage or
tarragon**
1 teaspoon sea salt
1 teaspoon black pepper
1 cup whipping cream
Butter (optional)

Preheat the oven to 300°F. Grease a 9-inch square baking pan.

Season the yam and onion with the lovage and salt and pepper. Layer the slices in the prepared baking pan. Spoon a small amount of the cream over each layer, reserving most of the cream for the top.

Cover with aluminum foil and bake for 45 – 60 minutes or until the yams are tender throughout. Remove the foil for the last 15 minutes.

If desired, dot with butter and broil for a few minutes to achieve a rich, golden color.

Yield: 4 side-dish servings

ABOVE: *The West Coast cuisine of chef Rodney J. Butters features local seafood, fish, and vegetables, savored with a range of regional wines.*

Ocean Pointe Resort Hotel & Spa

*C*ricket. Lawn bowling. Fish and chips in dark-paneled pubs. High tea featuring scones and cucumber sandwiches. Shopping for tartans and bone china.

Victoria,
British Columbia

(800) 667-4677

$$

spa

This may not be England, but it's certainly English — or at least English with a Pacific flair. Beautiful Victoria, on Vancouver Island, has a charm all its own, with magnificent sea vistas, sophisticated dining, and international shopping.

Ocean Pointe Resort Hotel & Spa, located on the Inner Harbour, is an excellent base from which to take in everything Victoria has to offer. Light and airy, decorated in coral hues and earth tones, the hotel boasts some of the best views of Victoria. It directly overlooks the Parliament Buildings across the harbor.

Although Ocean Pointe has plenty of serious activity, from a business center for its corporate clients to a full fitness facility for those who might have a different definition of a power lunch, it coddles every guest equally. The Spa offers aromatherapy, facials, micronized algae body wraps, and other relaxing and rejuvenating treatments.

And after an active day of whale watching or sightseeing in Victoria, guests are apt to return to the hotel to relish a candlelit meal at The Victorian, the fine dining restaurant. Here harbor views must compete with a West Coast cuisine that's designed to be low-calorie and low-sodium, using the freshest ingredients from British Columbia's bounty. For al fresco dining, The Boardwalk Restaurant specializes in regional dishes. Entertainment options include Rick's Lounge and Piano Bar.

ABOVE: *This city resort is an excellent base from which to explore charming Victoria.*

AT A GLANCE: *250 rooms and 32 suites, all with harbor view, some with private balcony/patio; 1 suite with Jacuzzi, fireplace, private balcony/patio, harbor view. 2 restaurants, fitness center, spa, sauna, whirlpool, beauty salon, indoor pool, day/night tennis, whale watching.* NEARBY: *shops, movie theaters, golf, bicycling, rollerblading, hiking, nature walking, horseback riding, beach, scuba diving, snorkeling, windsurfing, boating, marina, fishing, skating.*

Dungeness Crab and Fennel Roulade

This roulade can be presented whole or pre-sliced. Ocean Pointe serves it with truffle and fly fish caviar (see recipe) and baby salad greens in a vinaigrette.

12 ounces fresh Dungeness crabmeat, cooked
4 ounces fennel, blanched, julienned
1 tablespoon finely chopped chervil
1 tablespoon finely chopped lemon balm
1 tablespoon finely diced red bell pepper
1 tablespoon finely diced yellow bell pepper
1 tablespoon lime juice
1 tablespoon olive oil
½ teaspoon crushed black pepper
4 (6-inch round) pieces of rice paper, soaked in warm water until soft

Mix the crabmeat, fennel, chervil, lemon balm, diced bell pepper, lime juice, oil, and black pepper.

Lay the rice paper flat and pat dry. Place some of the crab mixture on each piece of rice paper and roll up. Either fold in or trim the ends.

Yield: 4 appetizer servings

Truffle and Fly Fish Caviar

½ cup white balsamic vinegar
1½ cups olive oil
1 tablespoon fresh lime juice
2 teaspoons finely chopped shallot
1 small black truffle (canned), finely chopped
2 teaspoons caviar (see note)
1 teaspoon finely chopped chervil
1 teaspoon finely chopped lemon balm
Salt and crushed black pepper to taste

Whisk the vinegar, oil, and lime juice. Stir in the shallot, truffle, caviar, chervil, and lemon balm; add the salt and pepper.

Serve with the Dungeness crab and fennel roulade.

Note: For this recipe, Ocean Pointe uses fly fish caviar, which is available in Japanese markets or specialty food shops.

Yield: 4 appetizer servings

. . . .
BELOW: *The Victorian, Ocean Pointe's fine dining restaurant, features harbor views and savory dishes.*

Chateau Whistler Resort

L ocated a two-hour drive from Vancouver, Whistler keeps die-hard skiers happy nearly year round. Glacier skiing extends the regular winter-spring season to the end of August.

*Whistler,
British Columbia*

(800) 606-8244

$$

golf / mountain / spa

Hortsman Glacier on Blackcomb Mountain is the site of Whistler's summer runs, suitable for both intermediate and advanced skiers.

Chateau Whistler is a deluxe resort that indulges guests with every creature comfort in an alpine atmosphere. It has become a popular destination for cross-country skiing as well. During the warmer months guests enjoy fly fishing, mountain biking, heli-hiking, and hot-air ballooning. Golfers choose from three courses, including the Chateau Whistler course designed by Robert Trent Jones, Jr., that features mountain streams and rocky ledges — golfers ascend more than three hundred feet during the game.

After a day of golfing or engaging in myriad alpine pursuits, a relaxing massage or a face and body treatment may be in order. At Chateau Whistler a brand new spa awaits.

Not least among Chateau Whistler's attractions is fine dining. The Wildflower Restaurant features fresh local produce for breakfast, lunch, afternoon tea, and dinner. The Mallard Bar, which offers a view of Blackcomb Mountain, serves cocktails, appetizers, and desserts to the strains of live piano music.

Just steps away, the village of Whistler lies nestled in the Coast Mountains. Here in the splendor of the Pacific coast, hikers find moss-covered trails, massive pines, and abundant wildlife. The region, a trout fishing paradise, is dotted with cold-water lakes and roaring mountain streams. The catch-and-release system ensures that the trout, like Whistler's other natural resources, will be here for future vacationers to enjoy. Guests can be assured the black bears that stretch lazily in the sun on the slopes of Whistler Mountain, the rainbow trout that glisten in the clear mountain streams, and the stands of rustling aspens will be here to greet them on their return visits.

ABOVE: *This year-round destination offers everything from downhill skiing to mountain biking — along with an unlimited supply of pure mountain air.*

AT A GLANCE: *516 rooms and 47 suites, many with Jacuzzi, hot tub, fireplace, scenic view. 2 restaurants, fitness center, spa, steam room, sauna, whirlpool, shops, supervised children's programs, indoor / outdoor (heated) pool, tennis, golf.* NEARBY: *cooking courses, beauty salon, movie theaters, indoor tennis, bicycling, rollerblading, hiking, nature walking, horseback riding, beach, watersports, windsurfing, boating, river rafting, fishing, downhill / cross-country skiing, snowboarding, skating, snowshoeing, snowmobiling, sleigh rides.*

Nine-Spice Roast Duck

Chateau Whistler's chefs suggest that this dish be served with a selection of cooked vegetables such as bok choy, shiitake mushrooms, and Anaheim chilies.

Nine-Spice Marinade:
1 teaspoon 5-spice powder (see note)
1 teaspoon sesame oil
1 tablespoon vegetable oil
1 garlic clove, finely chopped
1 tablespoon finely chopped ginger
2 tablespoons hoisin sauce
1 tablespoon dark cane sugar
1 tablespoon finely minced lemon grass
   (see note)
1 star anise, ground (see note)
2 pinches of white pepper
2 pinches of black pepper
2 pinches of salt

Duck:
6 pieces of boneless fresh duck breast
Vegetable oil

Glaze:
1 tablespoon finely chopped shallot
Olive oil
3 ounces Chardonnay
4 cups roast duck (or chicken) stock,
   reduced to 3 ounces
2 tablespoons Shanghai honey
   (see note) or regular honey
¼ cup butter
Salt and white pepper to taste

Potatoes:
1 garlic bulb
1½ pounds sweet potatoes, peeled
   and cut into 2-inch cubes
1½ pounds Idaho baking potatoes,
   peeled and cut into 2-inch cubes

Olive oil
Butter
1 cup scalded milk
Salt and white pepper to taste
Pinch of nutmeg

Garnish:
Sprigs of cilantro or pea sprouts

Prepare the marinade and the duck. Combine all the marinade ingredients and rub the duck liberally with it. Refrigerate for 8 hours or overnight.

Place the duck skin side down in an oiled medium-hot pan to render the fat from under the skin.

Prepare the glaze. Sauté the shallot in a hot, oiled pan. Add the wine and reduce by 70 percent. Add the stock and honey and bring to a low boil. Remove from heat and whisk in the butter. Season.

Prepare the potatoes. Preheat the oven to 400°F. Rub the garlic and the potatoes with a small amount of the oil. Roast, turning occasionally, until golden brown and fully baked. Remove the roasted cloves from the garlic bulb and reserve. Sauté 3 or 4 of the cloves in the butter. Add the potato and mash. Adjust the taste and consistency with the milk, butter, and seasoning. Cover and keep warm in the oven or in a water bath.

Finish cooking the duck. Preheat the oven to 425°F and roast for a few minutes, skin side down. Brush with honey and let rest for a few minutes. Slice with a straight ⅛-inch cut across the breast.

Place a large spoonful of potato on each plate. Cover with the duck slices. Drizzle the glaze around the plate but not over the meat. Garnish with a sprig of cilantro or pea sprouts.

Note: 5-spice powder, lemon grass, star anise, and Shanghai honey are available in Asian markets.

Yield: 6 servings

Emerald Lake Lodge

Emerald Lake Lodge simply defines the term "mountain retreat," whether you're looking for a winter interlude in front of a cozy log fire or a summer escape surrounded by wildflower-dotted fields.

Yoho National Park, British Columbia

(800) 663-6336 or (604) 343-6321

$

mountain

The lodge, located a 20-minute drive from Lake Louise, was constructed in 1902 on a 13-acre peninsula jutting into glacial Emerald Lake. It was renovated as a deluxe year-round retreat in 1986.

The historic lodge remains the heart of the resort. Built of hand-hewn timber and birch, it includes massive stone fireplaces, a formal dining room, a games room, and spacious verandas. The Kicking Horse Bar features an oak bar transplanted from an 1890s saloon in Canada's northern Yukon Territory. The 85 guest units, located in 24 cabin-like buildings, boast fieldstone fireplaces, twig furniture, and decks overlooking the green waters of the aptly named Emerald Lake.

Emerald Lake Lodge's Rocky Mountain cuisine has attracted a great deal of attention in the gourmet world. Recently Bonnie Stern, a well-known Canadian cookbook author and cooking instructor, offered classes here.

At the Mount Burgess dining room, guests begin their meal with the Rocky Mountain game platter. The theme continues with such main-course offerings as West Coast salmon with wontons, vegetables, and miso broth, baby arctic char with potatoes over green beans, hazelnuts, and pancetta, or grilled Alberta beef tenderloin with port wine and shoestring potatoes. Bumbleberry pie with Winnipeg cream cheese sorbet and warm apple crisp with maple ice cream are two of the creative conclusions.

In summer, the Mount Burgess dining room serves afternoon tea on the veranda, while the Cilantro on the Lake restaurant offers light fare daily.

One of the highlights of Emerald Lake Lodge is its hiking and cross-country ski trails. In winter, guests are shuttled to the Lake Louise ski area. In summer, fossil enthusiasts from around the world come to inspect the Burgess Shale on Mount Burgess, which overlooks the lodge. But perhaps the biggest draws of Emerald Lake Lodge are its breathtaking views and its secluded setting.

ABOVE: The century-old lodge cocoons its guests in warmth and comfort.

AT A GLANCE: *85 rooms with fireplace, private balcony / patio, some with mountain / lake view. 2 restaurants, cooking courses, sauna, hiking, nature walking.* NEARBY: *fitness center, spa, beauty salon, shops, movie theaters, indoor / outdoor (heated) pool, tennis, golf, bicycling, horseback riding, downhill / cross-country skiing, snowboarding, skating, snowshoeing, dogsledding, sleigh rides.*

Caribou Medallions with Creamed Leeks and Wild Blueberry-Thyme Sauce

Wild Blueberry-Thyme Sauce:
¾ cup dark game stock (available in
   specialty food shops)
¼ cup dry red wine
2 tablespoons chopped thyme
4 tablespoons chopped shallot
1 tablespoon minced garlic
⅓ cup blueberries

Creamed Leeks:
1 leek (white part only), cut into thin
   strips
Clarified butter
2 tablespoons dry white wine
2 tablespoons whipping cream
Salt and pepper

Squash-Potato Purée:
2 tablespoons whipping cream
Grated nutmeg to taste
½ pound butternut squash, unpeeled,
   roasted (see note)
¼ potato, boiled

Caribou:
8 (2-ounce) caribou medallions
Salt and pepper to taste
Clarified butter

Garnish:
4 sprigs of thyme

Prepare the sauce. Combine all the ingredients in a saucepan and simmer for 10 – 15 minutes or until reduced by three quarters. It should have a lustrous shine.

Prepare the leeks. Sauté the leeks in the clarified butter until tender. Deglaze the pan with the wine and add the cream. Reduce by three quarters. Season well with salt and pepper.

Prepare the squash-potato purée. Warm the cream in a shallow pan. Add the nutmeg. Purée the squash and the potato and add the cream. Season.

Prepare the caribou. Flatten the medallions with a mallet to a thickness of ¼ inch. Season with salt and pepper and sauté in the butter for 3 – 4 minutes or until medium rare.

To serve, place the creamed leeks and the squash-potato purée on each plate. Fan the caribou medallions on the plate and pour the sauce over them. Garnish with a sprig of thyme.

Note: To roast squash, cut in half and season the flesh and outer skin with salt and pepper. Place in a pan with 2 inches of water and cover with foil. Bake in a preheated 350°F oven for 40 minutes.

Yield: 4 servings

Above: *Emerald Lake Lodge simply defines the term "mountain retreat."*

Algonquin Hotel

*O*ne of the East Coast's top resorts is also one of its oldest. "The Watering Place of the Dominion," as the hilltop Algonquin Hotel was known, dates back to 1889.

St. Andrews-By-the-Sea, New Brunswick

(800) 441-1414

$

golf

In the early days, guests of the hotel paid just $3 per night for accommodation and meals when they came to the resort for its salt-water baths, seeking relief for whatever ailed them.

Today's St. Andrews-By-the-Sea vacationers enjoy a level of luxury never dreamed of by their predecessors. Guests of the Algonquin Hotel are treated to all the comforts and amenities of a modern resort along with the attractions of a natural environment. Here, you'll find an abundance of wildlife to observe, as well as hunting, fishing, canoeing, and sea kayaking.

Golf, however, ranks as *the* main activity at this bustling resort. The world-renowned 18-hole Seaside Course offers breathtaking ocean views along with rolling fairways. The nine-hole Woodland Course also draws many competitors.

The Algonquin's four restaurants feature the cuisine of Atlantic Canada. Favorite regional dishes served at this resort blend the bounty of the sea — such as clams, oysters, mussels, salmon, lobster — with the fruits of the land — such as fiddleheads and blueberries. Passamaquoddy Veranda, the main dining room, affords views of the front gardens and is especially famous for its bountiful Sunday brunch. The Algonquin Green, at the golf clubhouse, features light fare, while The Library serves as a café by day and a piano lounge by night. The lively Dockside pub has an unmistakably maritime flavor.

ABOVE: *For more than a century travelers have been coming to this resort for its scenery as well as its restorative waters and challenging golf.*

AT A GLANCE: *263 rooms with sea/garden view; 61 suites with sea/garden view, some with Jacuzzi, fireplace. 4 restaurants, cooking courses, fitness center, sauna, whirlpool, shops, supervised children's programs, outdoor (heated) pool, tennis, golf, golf clinics, bicycling, beach.* NEARBY: *movie theaters, hiking, nature walking, horseback riding, hunting, watersports, scuba diving, boating, marina, fishing, whale watching, sea kayaking, skating, historic walking tours, garden tours.*

Lobster Cakes with Marinated Tomatoes and Basil Oil

Marinated Tomatoes:
5 tablespoons balsamic vinegar
2 tablespoons olive oil
4 basil leaves
Salt and pepper to taste
16 cherry tomatoes

Lobster Cakes:
1 (2-pound) lobster, cooked
2 large potatoes, boiled and mashed
3 basil leaves, finely chopped
2 tablespoons mayonnaise
Salt and pepper to taste
All-purpose flour
1 egg, beaten
Fine bread crumbs
Light oil

Garnish:
Basil leaves
Basil oil (available in specialty food
   shops)

Prepare the marinated tomatoes. Combine the vinegar, oil, basil leaves, and salt and pepper. Marinate the tomatoes in the mixture for 15 minutes.

Prepare the lobster cakes. Remove the meat from the shell and cut into medium-sized cubes. Combine with the mashed potato, basil, mayonnaise, and salt and pepper. Shape the mixture into 8 cakes.

Dip each cake in the flour, then the egg, then the bread crumbs. Deep fry in the oil. Keep warm.

Serve the lobster cakes over the marinated tomatoes, garnished with basil leaves and basil oil.

Yield: 8 servings

ABOVE: *The Algonquin Hotel specializes in the cuisine of Atlantic Canada.*

Deerhurst Resort

I t's time to play in the mud. Whether your interest is spa treatments or off-road vehicles, Deerhurst has the mud for you. Dead Sea Mud treatment is just one of many options available at The Spa at Deerhurst, which offers special programs for stress reduction and body rejuvenation.

Huntsville, Ontario

(800) 461-4393

$

golf / spa

For some visitors, however, rejuvenation might mean jumping aboard a 4X4 vehicle for some off-road excitement under the guidance of a trained instructor. The 4X4 Adventures half-day program consists of some training followed by a two-hour trail ride across steep rock and through muddy forests.

Those with slightly more sedentary pursuits in mind are likely to choose Deerhurst for its excellent golf. The Deerhurst Highlands Golf Course, this resort's newest, incorporates natural features such as dense woods, winding creeks, and granite outcroppings. The Deerhurst Lakeside Golf Course, on the shores of Peninsula Lake, is often used for instruction. A seven-acre practice range offers private lessons with resort pros to help guests shave a few strokes off their game. Deerhurst keeps golfers in the action year round, thanks to an indoor practice range open November through May.

Deerhurst's three restaurants highlight regional produce and showcase the artistry of executive chef Roger Tremblay. Tremblay's signature dish, warm maple-smoked duck salad (see recipe opposite), reflects his interest in local foods prepared country-style.

Deerhurst is located in Huntsville, a two-and-a-half-hour drive north of Toronto.

ABOVE: *Guests of this resort can expect challenging golf, rejuvenating spa treatments, and even off-road excitement.*

AT A GLANCE: *111 rooms with whirlpool, fireplace, private balcony / patio, lake / golf course view; 249 suites and 360 condo / suite units with whirlpool, Jacuzzi, fireplace, private balcony / patio, lake / golf course view. 3 restaurants, cooking courses (part of theme weekends), fitness center, spa, steam room, sauna, whirlpool, beauty salon, shops, supervised children's programs, indoor / outdoor (heated) pool, indoor / outdoor / night tennis, squash, racquetball, golf, bicycling, hiking, nature walking, horseback riding, beach, watersports, windsurfing, boating, fishing, cross-country skiing, skating, snowmobiling, dogsledding, sleigh rides. NEARBY: movie theaters, rollerblading, marina, hunting, downhill skiing, snowboarding.*

Maple-Sap Pea Soup

1 pound whole yellow peas
1 piece ham knuckle
3 quarts maple sap (see note)
¼ cup maple syrup
½ cup diced carrot
¼ cup diced celery
½ cup diced onion
½ cup diced Black Forest ham
1 bay leaf
1 sprig of thyme
1 sprig of parsley
Salt and pepper to taste

Soak the peas in water for 1 – 2 hours.

Make a stock using the ham and the maple sap. Simmer for 1 hour, then strain out the ham knuckle, reserving the liquid. Add the peas and the remaining ingredients and cook over low heat for 1 – 2 hours or until the peas are tender (the soup should be thick). Season.

Note: An additional ¼ cup of maple syrup and 3 quarts of water can be substituted for the maple sap.

Yield: 8 servings

Warm Maple-Smoked Duck Salad

4 Boston lettuce leaves
4 radicchio leaves
4 Belgian endive leaves
8 ounces mesclun (enough greens to
    cover 4 salad plates)
6 tablespoons olive oil
1 shallot, finely diced
6 shiitake mushrooms, stems removed,
    thinly sliced
1 breast of maple-smoked duck, thinly
    sliced
2 tablespoons raspberry vinegar
1 tablespoon maple syrup
Salt and pepper to taste
1 tablespoon crushed black
    peppercorns

Place one each of the Boston, radicchio, and endive leaves on each plate. Arrange the mesclun greens on top. Try to give height to the plate, as the warm dressing will quickly wilt the greens.

Pour the oil into a hot sauté pan and sauté the shallot until transparent. Add the mushrooms and the duck slices and sauté until the duck is heated throughout. Leave the duck in the pan. Add the vinegar and maple syrup and bring to a boil. Add salt and pepper to taste.

Quickly arrange the duck slices over the greens. Pour the warm dressing over all and sprinkle with the crushed black peppercorns. Serve immediately, before the greens wilt.

Yield: 4 appetizer servings (or
    2 entrée servings)

. . . .
BELOW: *Deerhurst Resort executive chef Roger Tremblay enjoys using regional specialties, such as maple products.*

Château Mont Tremblant

The newest member of the Canadian Pacific Hotels family combines the French-inspired architecture of Québec with mountain ruggedness, for a getaway that both indulges and challenges.

Mont Tremblant, Québec

(800) 441-1414

$$

mountain

The $57-million Château Mont Tremblant may be a recent construction, but it is evocative of a 19th-century château. Its chimneys, pitched roofs, corrugated shingling, and stucco exteriors recall the residential architecture of rural Provence. The theme carries over to the interiors, which feature inlaid stone floors, cast-iron chandeliers, and warm woods, enhanced by the addition of Québec antiques.

Most of the 62 suites at this resort are fitted with fully equipped kitchens. For all its attention to the creature comforts, though, a rugged region lies just steps from the doors of the Château.

During the winter months, downhill skiing is the main attraction. This resort has been named the number one ski resort in eastern North America by *Ski Magazine*. In fact, the Mont Tremblant area has long been acknowledged to be the prime skiing locale east of the Rockies. Cross-country skiing, snowshoeing, snowmobiling, dogsledding, ice fishing, and ice climbing keep other guests busy. More reflective visitors can strap on a pair of snowshoes and follow a resort biologist into the Laurentian forest to observe white-tailed deer.

In the warm-weather months, the activity level never drops. Special events, from bike tours to blues festivals to classical music concerts, are scheduled all summer long.

Château Mont Tremblant's restaurants highlight the French ancestry of this region's inhabitants. The Windigo restaurant offers an à la carte menu, daily buffet, and Sunday brunch, while the Wigwam Café serves fast fare for those eager to hit the slopes. Not far from the resort, refined dishes are served at Aux Truffles, regional French cuisine at La Savoie, and traditional favorites at Crêperie Catherine.

ABOVE: *Both indoors and out, Château Mont Tremblant is evocative of a 19th-century château.*

AT A GLANCE: *254 rooms with lake/mountain/village view; 62 suites with lake/mountain/village view, 1 with Jacuzzi, fireplace. 2 restaurants, cooking courses, fitness center, spa, steam room, sauna, whirlpool, beauty salon, shops, movie theaters, supervised children's programs, indoor/outdoor (heated) pool, day/ night tennis, golf, bicycling, rollerblading, hiking, nature walking, horseback riding, beach, scuba diving, snorkeling, windsurfing, boating, marina, fishing, downhill/cross-country skiing, snowboarding, skating, snowshoeing, snowmobiling, dogsledding, sleigh rides. NEARBY: 3 restaurants, hot-air ballooning, river rafting, hunting.*

Noisette of Deer with Gelée de Sapin Venison Sauce

The Château Mont Tremblant chefs serve this dish with baked apples garnished with red-wine jelly, wild mushrooms sautéed in butter, and pommes maximes (see note 1).

½ cup wine vinegar

5 cups dry red wine

2 tablespoons chopped parsley

4 sprigs of thyme

1 bay leaf

20 black peppercorns

2 cloves

2 carrots, thinly sliced

½ medium onion, thinly sliced

5 shallots, thinly sliced

1 celery stalk, diced

4 (6-ounce) noisettes of deer, trimmed

2 teaspoons gelée de sapin (see note 2)

1 cup red port

4 cups game demi-glace (available in specialty food shops) or veal stock

¼ cup butter

Salt and pepper to taste

Olive oil or goose fat

Make a marinade by heating the vinegar and mixing it with the wine, parsley, thyme, bay leaf, peppercorns, cloves, carrot, onion, shallot, and celery. Marinate the meat, in the refrigerator, for at least 24 hours, preferably 48 hours.

Remove the meat and drain on paper towels. Add the fir jelly, port, and demi-glace to the marinade and reduce over medium heat until thick enough to nicely coat the meat. Add the butter and salt and pepper.

Heat a small amount of the oil in a sauté pan. Cook the meat for 2 minutes on each side (it should be pinkish and soft, and will be more tender if set aside for a few minutes after it is cooked).

To serve, place a noisette on each plate and cover with the sauce. Serve hot.

Note 1: Pommes maximes are thinly sliced potatoes arranged in a floral design and cooked with butter, salt, and pepper in a 420°F oven for 4 minutes.

Note 2: Gelée de sapin, available in specialty food shops in certain regions, is a jelly made from the resin of the fir tree.

Yield: 4 servings

. . . .

BELOW: *This year-round Laurentian resort combines mountain ruggedness with the French-inspired architecture of Québec.*

UNITED STATES

Blaine
Seattle
WA Spokane
Portland
Sunriver
Eugene
OR
ID
MT
ND
MN
WI
ME
VT
Lake Placid
NH
NY
MA
CT
RI
Southbury
New York City
PA
MD
DE
NJ

Sheridan
Jackson Hole
WY
Cheyenne
SD
Kohler
Milwaukee
MI
OH
WV
VA

CA
NV
Salt Lake City
Snowbird
Provo
Steamboat Springs
NE
IA
IL
IN
Kansas City
St. Louis
KY
NC

San Francisco
Carmel
UT
Vail/
Vail Valley
Keystone
Colorado Springs
CO
KS
MO
Ridgedale
Lakeview
TN

Ojai
Los Angeles
Palm Springs/
La Quinta
Carlsbad
San Diego
Wickenburg
AZ
Carefree
Scottsdale
Phoenix
Santa Fe
Albuquerque
NM
Tucson
OK
AR
Little Rock
Atlanta
SC
GA
Savannah

MS
AL
Ft. Worth
Dallas/
Irving
LA
Panama City
Beach
Jacksonville
Sea Island
Amelia Island
FL
Orlando
Tampa

TX
Austin
Houston
San Antonio

Miami/
Coral Gables
Florida Keys
(Little Torch Key,
Longboat Key)

Hawaii
Honolulu
Kohala Coast
(Island of Hawaii)

AL:	Alabama	KS:	Kansas	NE:	Nebraska	TN:	Tennessee
AR:	Arkansas	KY:	Kentucky	NH:	New Hampshire	TX:	Texas
AZ:	Arizona	LA:	Louisiana	NJ:	New Jersey	UT:	Utah
CA:	California	MA:	Massachusetts	NM:	New Mexico	VA:	Virginia
CO:	Colorado	MD:	Maryland	NV:	Nevada	VT:	Vermont
CT:	Connecticut	ME:	Maine	NY:	New York	WA:	Washington
DE:	Delaware	MI:	Michigan	OH:	Ohio	WI:	Wisconsin
FL:	Florida	MN:	Minnesota	OK:	Oklahoma	WV:	West Virginia
GA:	Georgia	MO:	Missouri	OR:	Oregon	WY:	Wyoming
IA:	Iowa	MS:	Mississippi	PA:	Pennsylvania		
ID:	Idaho	MT:	Montana	RI:	Rhode Island		
IL:	Illinois	NC:	North Carolina	SC:	South Carolina		
IN:	Indiana	ND:	North Dakota	SD:	South Dakota		

OPPOSITE: *The Dunes is one of four challenging golf courses at La Quinta Resort & Club near Palm Springs, California.*

The Boulders

*L*ocated just north of Scottsdale, The Boulders lives up to its name, nestled among giant granite formations. These boulders form a dramatic introduction to this Sonoran Desert locale.

Carefree, Arizona

(800) 553-1717 or (602) 488-9009

$$$$

golf / tennis

The 12-million-year-old boulders scattered throughout the property complement the unique architecture of this resort, whose individual guest casitas with wood-beamed ceiling echo the colors of the desert.

Along with its outstanding architecture, The Boulders has received much attention for its golf and tennis facilities. Two championship courses designed by Jay Moorish offer 36 holes of golf. Like the resort itself, these courses incorporate features of the surrounding desert landscape. Granite boulders, saguaro cacti, and mesquite and palo verde trees have been integrated into the design.

Tennis buffs will find six plexi-cushioned tennis courts as well as a pro shop and two full-time pros, who offer private lessons as well as weekly clinics. Every Saturday, the resort hosts The Boulders Challenge, a doubles match that pits guests against the pros.

The Sonoran Spa at The Boulders uses desert plants in its many soothing treatments. Aloe, yucca, and sage have been selected for their natural healing properties. Guests can choose from Swedish massage, aromatherapy, reflexology, aloe wrap, desert springs exfoliation, and facials.

For some visitors, the best pampering comes in the form of a rewarding meal at the end of the day. The Boulders has a variety of restaurants, including Latilla, which serves American cuisine in a Southwestern atmosphere. The Palo Verde, which features a display kitchen, offers seafood and regional specialties. The Boulders Club serves both lunch and dinner on its terrace, with views of the Sonoran foothills and the golf course as a backdrop. Other choices include the Sunshine Juice Bar for healthy and refreshing snacks, The Bakery Café for chocolate pastries, and Cantina del Pedregal for Southwestern dishes. Desert views are a principal attraction at the Discovery Lounge, a nightspot.

ABOVE: *Giant granite formations provide a dramatic introduction to this Sonoran Desert locale.*

AT A GLANCE: *160 casitas with fireplace, private balcony / patio, mountain / desert / golf course view; 3 suites; 35 villas. 5 restaurants, cooking courses, fitness center, spa, steam room, sauna, whirlpool, beauty salon, shops, supervised children's programs (holidays only), outdoor (heated) pool, tennis, golf, touring / off-road bicycling, hiking, nature walking, hot-air ballooning, rock climbing, jeep tours, museum.* NEARBY: *rollerblading, horseback riding, river rafting, fishing, hunting, Grand Canyon tours.*

Orange Angel Food Cake with Warm Berry Compote

Orange Angel Food Cake:

2 cups sugar

1⅓ cups cake flour

2 cups egg whites (from about 16 large eggs)

½ teaspoon cream of tartar

⅛ teaspoon salt

1 tablespoon finely grated orange zest

¼ teaspoon vanilla

Berry Compote:

1 teaspoon cornstarch

¼ cup water

2 pints strawberries, hulled and quartered

2 tablespoons orange-flavored liqueur

1 tablespoon sugar

1 pint blueberries

Preheat the oven to 375°F.

Prepare the angel food cake. In a large bowl, sift ¾ cup of the sugar and the flour three times.

Using an electric mixer at medium speed, whip the egg whites for 1 minute or until foamy. Add the cream of tartar and salt and whip for 1 more minute. Increase the speed to high and gradually beat in the remaining 1¼ cups of sugar and continue to beat until the mixture is stiff and smooth; do not overbeat.

Using a large rubber spatula, gently fold the egg white mixture into the dry mixture. Stir in the orange zest and vanilla.

Turn the batter into an ungreased 10-inch tube pan with a removable bottom. Smooth over the top. Run a knife gently through the center of the batter to remove any large air bubbles. Bake for 45 minutes or until the top springs back when lightly pressed and a cake tester inserted in the center comes out clean. Invert the pan over a narrow-necked bottle (to help keep the cake above the surface of the table) and cool completely. Turn the pan right side up and run a thin, sharp knife around the sides and center of the pan to loosen the cake. Lift the cake out of the rim by the tube. Cut around the bottom of the cake to loosen it, turn the cake upside down, and remove the bottom of the pan.

Prepare the berry compote. In a small bowl, dissolve the cornstarch in the water. Heat a medium-sized non-reactive sauté pan (such as stainless steel or glass) over moderate heat. Add the strawberries, liqueur, and sugar. Stir in the dissolved cornstarch and cook for 2 minutes or until slightly thickened. Fold in the blueberries. Serve warm, with the orange angel food cake.

Note: The cake itself can be prepared up to 8 hours ahead; cover and let stand at room temperature.

Yield: 12 servings

. . . .

ABOVE: *Two championship golf courses at The Boulders mirror the surrounding desert terrain: saguaro cacti, mesquite and palo verde trees, and great hulks of granite.*

Marriott's Camelback Inn

Majestic Camelback Mountain, which resembles a resting camel, dominates the Phoenix area with magnificent red rocks set against the desert horizon.

Scottsdale, Arizona

(800) 228-9290

$$

golf/spa

Marriott's Camelback Inn enjoys a view of the famous landmark. Located at the base of Mummy Mountain, this deluxe resort pampers and pleases its guests with fine dining, championship golf, and exhilarating spa treatments. Camelback is the only Arizona resort to earn Mobil Five Star and AAA Five Diamond awards and has been named Marriott's Hotel of the Year, nationwide.

For all its desert beauty and sprawling facilities, this resort is located just a 10-minute drive from Phoenix Sky Harbor Airport. The convenient location has long made Marriott's Camelback Inn popular with vacationers who have only a few days to squeeze in some rest and relaxation. For many of these travelers, golf is the magnet. Marriott's Camelback Golf Club offers two scenic championship courses, Padre and Indian Bend, and golfers can take advantage of instruction by PGA professionals on staff. This club is also home to the innovative John Jacobs Practical Golf schools.

For others, The Spa at Camelback Inn is reason in itself to visit this desert getaway. This large European-style spa features exercise facilities, a full-service salon, nutritional counseling, wellness programs, and a complete range of spa treatments: aromatherapy, shiatsu, Swedish massage, reflexology, Thalassotherapy, full-body mud mask, clay treatments, and facials.

The Spa has its own health-conscious restaurant, Sprouts. Diners might start with a smoothie and continue with Arizona-inspired dishes such as vegetarian chili (see recipe opposite), seared shrimp and pan-roasted vegetables with lemon-pepper linguine in garlic broth, or barbecued chicken pizza with eggplant fennel, oven-roasted garlic, and golden tomato sauce. Other dining choices at the resort include The Chaparral, serving Continental cuisine, and The Navajo, featuring Arizona dishes, from fajitas to rack of lamb to fillet of Black Angus beef.

ABOVE: *After a game of golf or tennis, guests can cool off with a dip in the palm-shaded pool.*

AT A GLANCE: *427 rooms with private balcony/patio, mountain view; 27 suites with fireplace, private balcony/patio, mountain view. 6 restaurants, fitness center, spa, steam room, sauna, whirlpool, beauty salon, shops, supervised children's programs, outdoor (heated) pool, watersports, day/night tennis, golf, bicycling, rollerblading, hiking, nature walking.* NEARBY: *movie theaters, indoor pool, indoor tennis, horseback riding, hot-air ballooning, river rafting.*

Vegetarian Chili

This healthful dish is served at Sprouts restaurant, which is located in the spa at Marriott's Camelback Inn.

1 medium Spanish onion, diced
1 medium red bell pepper, seeded and diced
1 medium green bell pepper, seeded and diced
1 tablespoon olive oil
1 medium jicama, diced (see note)
1 medium zucchini, diced
1 medium yellow squash, diced
½ teaspoon ground cumin
½ teaspoon curry powder
½ teaspoon toasted dark chili powder
½ teaspoon chopped cilantro
Salt and white pepper to taste
1 cup diced tomato, canned, drained
½ cup pinto beans (cooked but slightly firm)
½ cup black beans (cooked but slightly firm)

Sauté the onion and bell pepper in the oil over high heat until translucent. Reduce heat to medium. Add the jicama and cook for 3 minutes. Add the zucchini and squash and cook for 2 minutes. Add the cumin, curry powder, chili powder, cilantro, and salt and pepper and cook, stirring, for 1 minute. Add the tomato and the beans and cook for 30 minutes. Serve hot.

Note: The jicama, often referred to as the Mexican potato, is a large, bulbous root vegetable with thin brown skin and crunchy white flesh. It is available fresh November through May in Mexican markets and many supermarkets.

Yield: 4 servings

Golden Gazpacho

Soup:
4 yellow tomatoes, coarsely chopped
4 cucumbers, peeled and coarsely chopped
2 green bell peppers, seeded and coarsely chopped
4 yellow bell peppers, seeded and coarsely chopped
1 red onion, chopped
1 garlic clove
1 cup V-8 brand vegetable juice
6 tablespoons red wine vinegar
¼ cup olive oil
Dash of Tabasco
Salt and pepper to taste

Garnish:
½ jicama, finely diced (see note under recipe opposite)
½ red bell pepper, seeded and finely diced
½ red onion, finely diced
4 teaspoons snipped chives
1 ounce cooked lump crabmeat

Combine all the soup ingredients in a blender or food processor and process until smooth. Refrigerate for at least 2 hours, preferably overnight.

To serve, sprinkle the garnish ingredients over the gazpacho in each soup bowl. Serve chilled.

Yield: 4 servings

BELOW: *Crouching at the base of Mummy Mountain, Marriott's Camelback Inn indulges: fine dining, championship golf, and invigorating spa treatments.*

Marriott's Mountain Shadows Resort and Golf Club

A t the Mountain Shadows you feel as though you've stepped into an oasis of pools and palm trees, with an abundance of good food and an easy-going style.

Scottsdale, Arizona

(800) 782-2123

$

golf/tennis

Although it is located just blocks from the larger Marriott's Camelback Inn, the atmosphere at this resort is completely different from that of its sister property. The Mountain Shadows, which was built in 1958, is one of Arizona's first resorts, and it faithfully retains its original relaxed mood. It continues to please guests who are prepared to sit back and enjoy a real desert vacation.

Like other Phoenix-area resorts, Marriott's Mountain Shadows Resort and Golf Club is noted for its superb golf facilities. The award-winning executive course spans more than 40 acres, so players are supplied with an electric cart when they're out on the links. Golfers also find a practice range, an award-winning full-service golf shop with equipment rentals, and lessons given by five teaching professionals. Shorts are permitted here, but cutoffs are not, and male golfers are required to wear collared shirts.

Tennis is another top draw at the Mountain Shadows. The Tennis Club features eight championship plexipave tennis courts, all lit for evening playing. Guests who want to brush up on their game will find a U.S. Professional Tennis Association member ready to help. Two free clinics are offered every week to resort guests only.

Dining is part of the Mountain Shadows experience. For lunch and dinner, Shells Oyster Bar and Seafood tempts the palate with 12 varieties of fresh fish daily. The Cactus Flower Café serves three meals a day. The Sunset Terrace offers al fresco dining with a view of the pool and Camelback Mountain. Golfers need never leave the links: The Bunkers Bar and Grill prepares hot and cold sandwiches, while The Country Club Restaurant serves a buffet breakfast and a light lunch between rounds.

ABOVE: *This pioneer resort in the Phoenix area faithfully retains its desert atmosphere.*

AT A GLANCE: *316 rooms with mountain view; 19 suites with private balcony/patio, mountain view. 5 restaurants, fitness center, spa, steam room, sauna, whirlpool, beauty salon, shops, supervised children's programs, outdoor (heated) pool, watersports, day/night tennis, golf, bicycling, rollerblading, hiking, nature walking.* NEARBY: *movie theaters, indoor pool, indoor tennis, horseback riding, hot-air ballooning, river rafting.*

Sweet-and-Spicy Crab Salad

This salad is served hot.

Orange-Cilantro Vinaigrette (yields 3 cups):
3 tablespoons chopped cilantro
½ cup orange juice concentrate, undiluted
½ cup apple cider vinegar
2 cups olive oil

Salad:
1 cup diced red onion
1 cup diced red bell pepper
¾ cup orange-cilantro vinaigrette
1 pound cooked crabmeat, diced large
1 cup peeled, seeded, diced cucumber
1 cup diced papaya
½ teaspoon black pepper
8 Belgian endive leaves
12 ounces spinach leaves
16 strips red bell pepper

Prepare the vinaigrette. Combine all the ingredients in a bowl and mix. Reserve ¾ cup in the refrigerator for this recipe and store the remainder in the refrigerator for later use.

Prepare the salad. Sauté the onion and bell pepper in the vinaigrette for 3 minutes. Add the crabmeat and sauté for 2 minutes. Add the cucumber, papaya, and black pepper and sauté for 20 seconds. Pour the mixture over the endive and spinach leaves.

Garnish each salad plate with 4 strips of red bell pepper and serve immediately.

Yield: 4 servings

Avocado-Crab Relish

The Mountain Shadows chefs suggest this relish be served over fresh fish, instead of a sauce. It can also be used as a stuffing for artichoke bottoms or as an appetizer, served on crackers or focaccia flat bread.

8 ounces cooked crabmeat
½ avocado, pitted, peeled, and diced ¼ inch
¼ cup diced green bell pepper
¼ cup diced red bell pepper
¼ cup diced yellow bell pepper
¼ cup diced red onion
¼ cup sliced green onion
¼ cup red wine vinegar
¼ cup olive oil
¼ teaspoon salt
¼ teaspoon pepper

Mix all the ingredients.

Yield: 2 cups

· · · · · · · · ·
ABOVE: *Golf, tennis, and a sprawling pool ensure that guests of Marriott's Mountain Shadows are kept refreshed.*

Scottsdale Princess Arizona

Perched at the edge of the desert, the Scottsdale Princess Arizona is truly an oasis. Guests at this sprawling resort find no shortage of activities to occupy their time.

Scottsdale, Arizona

(800) 223-1818

$$$

golf

Whether your idea of fun is golf or gourmet dining, basketball or biking, you'll find it at this striking resort set against the rugged McDowell Mountains.

This AAA Five Diamond resort indulges its guests with luxury. Set on 450 acres, the Scottsdale Princess Arizona features Mexican Colonial architecture and colors that echo the shades of the desert.

The cuisine of this resort, which features four restaurants, also reflects its surroundings. The award-winning Marquesa serves Catalan dishes: tapas accompanied by fine Spanish wines, followed by entrées such as peppercorn-crusted tenderloin of beef with dried cherries and stuffed morels or grilled turbot and prawns with black olive and saffron sauce. La Hacienda, located in an historic ranch house, serves Mexican specialties such as roast suckling pig carved tableside, grilled seafood, and chicken and beef dishes. Here, strolling mariachis delight diners with their romantic ballads. Other dining options are Las Ventanas, for a taste of Arizona's Southwestern cuisine, and The Grill, at the golf clubhouse, for mesquite-grilled steaks, seafood, and prime rib.

The unique flavors of the Scottsdale Princess Arizona are the creation of a superb culinary staff headed by executive chef Reed Groban. Groban has elevated dining at this resort to its present high level; his dedication includes traveling to Spain and to many Mexican villages to research their cuisines firsthand.

ABOVE: *The hotel echoes the subtle shades of the desert.*

AT A GLANCE: *438 rooms and 68 villas with private balcony / patio, mountain / pool / golf course view; 75 suites and 69 casitas with fireplace, private balcony / patio, mountain / pool / golf course view. 4 restaurants, cooking courses, fitness center, spa, steam room, sauna, whirlpool, beauty salon, shops, supervised children's programs, outdoor (heated) pool, day / night tennis, golf, bicycling, rollerblading, hiking, watersports, fishing.* NEARBY: *movie theaters, nature walking, horseback riding, hot-air ballooning, boating, marina, river rafting, hunting, skating.*

Stuffed Ancho Chilies

Chilies:

4 ancho chilies (see note 1)

4 (5-ounce) chicken breasts, partially smoked or charcoal grilled, cubed

¼ serrano chili, seeded and chopped

¾ cup peeled and diced tomatoes

1½ cups grated Monterey Jack cheese

1 tablespoon lime juice

1½ garlic cloves, chopped

1 teaspoon chili powder

1 teaspoon minced ancho chili, seeded

2 tablespoons golden raisins

3 tablespoons julienned dried apricot

2 tablespoons julienned dried apple

Salt and pepper to taste

Chipotle Sauce:

1 cup chicken consommé

1 chipotle, minced (see note 2)

Salt and pepper to taste

¾ cup sour cream

Tomato-Carrot Sauce:

2 cups chicken consommé

3 medium carrots

2 large tomatoes, peeled, seeded, and halved

¼ tablespoon lime juice

Assembly:

Red and green mole sauces (optional) (available in Mexican markets or specialty food shops)

Cilantro leaves

Prepare the chilies. Steam the ancho chilies in a colander, in a covered pot over boiling water, for 2 minutes or until soft. Slit lengthwise and remove the seeds and membrane. Combine the remaining ingredients and use the mixture to stuff each ancho chili. Store covered in the refrigerator until 30 minutes before cooking time.

Prepare the chipotle sauce. Heat the consommé in a saucepan. Add the chipotle and cook until the consommé is reduced to a scant ⅔ cup. Season. Remove from heat and allow to cool, then slowly fold it into the sour cream. The sauce should be slightly rust-colored.

Prepare the tomato-carrot sauce. Heat the consommé in a saucepan. Add the carrots and tomato and simmer until very soft. Remove from heat and process in a food processor until smooth. Add the lime juice. Strain and keep warm over low heat.

Assemble the dish. Preheat the oven to 375°F. Put the chilies on an oiled baking sheet and bake until their internal temperature reaches 145°F. Meanwhile, slowly simmer both the chipotle sauce and the tomato-carrot sauce until hot; do not boil. Remove the chilies from the oven and place on a wire rack over a tray.

To serve, pour some tomato-carrot sauce on each plate. Coat a chili with the chipotle sauce and place in the center of the tomato-carrot sauce. If desired, drizzle with the prepared red and green mole sauces to add color. Garnish with a cilantro leaf.

Note 1: The sweetest of the dried chilies, the reddish-brown ancho chili (called a poblano in its fresh, green state) is 3 – 4 inches long. It is available in Mexican markets or specialty food shops.

Note 2: The chipotle is a dried, smoked jalapeño with wrinkled, dark brown skin. It can be purchased dried or canned in Mexican markets or specialty food shops.

Yield: 4 servings

SunBurst Resort

*S*unBurst embraces vacationers with a warm, "welcome to your desert home" kind of feeling. This resort may offer fewer on-site amenities than its mega-resort neighbors, but it provides rest and relaxation in a stylish package that never overwhelms.

Scottsdale, Arizona

(800) 528-7867

$$

golf

The SunBurst style becomes apparent as soon as you enter its spacious lobby, which combines flagstone, woven Indian fabrics, and a beamed ceiling for a Southwestern motif. This lobby is the perfect place for good conversation or a game of checkers by the crackling fire.

The Southwestern theme is also evident in SunBurst dining. The specialty of Rancho Saguaro is "cowboy fusion cuisine" — universal favorites with a Southwestern twist. Popular dishes include Southwestern tortilla soup with roast chicken and guacamole, crisp Maryland soft-shell crab sandwiches, seared Pacific salmon fillet, and grilled beef tenderloin. The display kitchen reveals that all dishes are prepared over Mexican red oak and pecan wood fires.

The vivid flames of the Rancho Saguaro kitchen are reflected in the colors of SunBurst's courtyard, which is the centerpiece of this resort. A recent $1-million landscaping project, part of a major renovation, has turned the courtyard into a showcase for native plants, from the towering saguaro to the squat barrel cacti, as well as bougainvillea and brilliant hibiscus. In the evening hours, outdoor fireplaces warm guests against the desert chill. The tall sandstone towers that cascade water into the freeform pool are fitted with flame torches, illuminating the night sky.

SunBurst is an excellent base from which to take in Phoenix-area attractions. These include 140 regional golf courses, desert jeep tours, hot-air balloon rides, and the art galleries of Old Town Scottsdale.

ABOVE: *The pool area is highlighted with native plants, from the soaring saguaro to the squat barrel cacti.*

AT A GLANCE: *205 rooms with private balcony/patio; 5 suites. Restaurant, fitness center, whirlpool, outdoor (heated) pool.* NEARBY: *cooking courses, spa, steam room, sauna, beauty salon, shops, movie theaters, supervised children's programs, indoor pool, indoor/outdoor/night tennis, golf, bicycling, rollerblading, hiking, nature walking, horseback riding, hot-air ballooning, beach, watersports, windsurfing, boating, river rafting, fishing, hunting, skating.*

Crab Cakes with Spicy Rémoulade

Spicy Rémoulade:
1 cup mayonnaise
4 sweet cornichons, finely diced
1 tablespoon capers
1 teaspoon cayenne
Juice of 1 lemon
1 teaspoon Worcestershire sauce
Salt and pepper to taste
Tabasco to taste

Crab Cakes:
1 pound jumbo lump crabmeat
2 eggs
½ cup mayonnaise
1 tablespoon chopped tarragon
4 extra-large shrimp, peeled and
    deveined
1 cup whipping cream
Salt to taste
1 teaspoon freshly ground black
    pepper
2 tablespoons snipped chives
1 tablespoon Dijon mustard

Prepare the rémoulade. Mix all the ingredients gently until they are well blended. Refrigerate.

Prepare the crab cakes. Mix the crabmeat, eggs, mayonnaise, and tarragon in a large bowl. Process the shrimp and cream in a food processor until thick. Fold into the crab mixture. Mix in the salt, pepper, chives, and mustard and form into cakes 1½ inches in diameter. Sear on a griddle until brown on both sides.

Serve the crab cakes with the spicy rémoulade.

Yield: 6 servings

. . . .
ABOVE: *A meal of crab cakes with spicy rémoulade is served poolside at SunBurst Resort's Rancho Saguaro restaurant.*

The Phoenician

. . . .

Gracing the base of Camelback Mountain, The Phoenician shines as one of the top resorts in a region known for its spectacular getaways.

. . . .

Scottsdale, Arizona

*(800) 888-8234 or
(800) 325-3589*

$$$

golf / spa / tennis

Decorated with a $1.7-million collection of artwork and antiques, this resort dazzles its guests with over-the-top opulence. Grand marble entrances. Splashing fountains. Scenic walks. Sprawling swimming pools. Spectacular desert vistas.

The Phoenician has chosen to complement rather than compete with those desert views. Along with lanky palms and lush greenery, the resort also exhibits native plants. Its two-acre Cactus Garden features more than 350 varieties of cacti and succulents, from both the Sonoran Desert and other arid regions of the world such as Africa and the Galapagos Islands. Guests can take a guided tour led by The Phoenician's resident horticulturist, or, alternatively, stroll along the wide trails on a self-conducted tour — which might offer the opportunity to see a hummingbird in one of the resort's many feeders or a lizard sunning itself atop a rock.

The Golf Club includes a 27-hole championship course as well as a driving range, putting green, and shop. The Tennis Garden features 12 courts, including an automated practice court. To cool down after a game, guests can take a dip in one of nine swimming pools with such added attractions as lagoons, waterfalls, and fountains. The fitness center and spa offers everything from aerobics to massage and various body treatments.

Diners have a wide choice of restaurants from which to choose. "What makes our dining establishments unique is the diversity of the cuisine," says James Cohen, executive chef at The Phoenician. Guests enjoy Mary Elaine's for modern French cuisine, The Terrace Dining Room for Italian dishes, and Windows on the Green for Southwestern cuisine. The Praying Monk offers intimate dining in a Renaissance-inspired salon. The Café & Ice Cream Parlor is the spot for casual eating. Other choices include the poolside Oasis, the Canyon Pool Grill, and the 19th Hole Snack Bar and Patio.

. . . .

ABOVE: The Cactus Garden features more than 350 varieties of cacti and succulents.

AT A GLANCE: *640 rooms with private balcony, mountain / desert / city view; 73 suites with private balcony, mountain / desert / city view, some with whirlpool, Jacuzzi, fireplace. 7 restaurants, cooking courses, fitness center, spa, steam room, sauna, whirlpool, beauty salon, shops, supervised children's programs, outdoor (heated) pool, watersports, day / night tennis, golf, bicycling, hiking, nature walking.* NEARBY: *movie theaters, rollerblading, horseback riding, hot-air ballooning, river rafting.*

Sauté of Foie Gras with Peppered Pineapple

1 tablespoon crushed coriander seed

1 tablespoon ground Sichuan pepper
(see note)

1 cup large pineapple chunks

Salt and pepper to taste

2 tablespoons duck fat or olive oil

2 teaspoons olive oil

1 teaspoon balsamic vinegar

2 cups mâche lettuce (also known as
corn salad), baby greens, or mesclun

2 teaspoons snipped chives

4 (3-ounce) foie gras medallions

8 pineapple leaves

2 teaspoons aged balsamic vinegar

Mix the coriander with the Sichuan pepper. Toss the pineapple in the mixture to coat, then season lightly with the salt and pepper. Scald over high heat in the hot duck fat until just golden brown on both sides. Keep at room temperature.

Mix the oil and vinegar. Toss the lettuce and chives in the mixture. Season with salt and pepper.

Season the foie gras with salt and pepper and sear in a very hot, dry (unoiled) pan.

To serve, place the tossed lettuce in the center of each plate. Top with the pineapple chunks, then the foie gras. Garnish with 2 of the pineapple leaves and drizzle with the aged balsamic vinegar. Serve hot.

Note: Sichuan (or Szechwan) pepper, a mildly hot spice, is available in Asian markets or specialty food shops.

Yield: 4 appetizer servings

. . . .

BELOW: *The Phoenician offers golf and tennis, and it has no fewer than nine swimming pools.*

Loews Ventana Canyon Resort

*L*ike a mountain lion crouching at the base of a jagged precipice, blending into its environment yet surveying all that surrounds it, Loews Ventana Canyon Resort keeps watch over the foothills of the Catalina Mountains.

Tucson, Arizona

(800) 234-5117

$ – $$$

golf

Dressed in the colors of the desert palette, the resort complements rather than clashes with the surrounding canyons, arroyos, and saguaros. Thrust into this terrain, its visitors are pampered, challenged, and ultimately rewarded with fine dining and deluxe accommodations.

The resort is well known for its two PGA championship golf courses. Both were designed by Tom Fazio, who has a home on the resort's signature hole: number three on the Mountain Course; this hole challenges players to literally shoot over the canyon.

Off the links, guests also find plenty of activity, from tennis to hiking to mountain biking. Luxurious spa treatments — massage, aromatherapy, facials, shiatsu, and a desert specialty called Hot Stones, which utilizes the comforting powers of heated rocks — help soothe newly awakened muscles. Nutrition/fitness counseling is also offered.

The beauty of the Sonoran Desert serves as a focal point for the resort. The lobby's flagstone floors lead to a wall of glass overlooking the saguaro-dotted hills and a waterfall that has carved a rocky canyon behind the resort. At the base of the falls, colorful koi swim in pools that in evening attract local wildlife and birdlife.

Evenings bring an elegant tone to the resort. Guests converge on the Ventana Room, which features gourmet American cuisine, an extensive wine list, and the lights of Tucson twinkling in the distance. For a rustic atmosphere, there's the new Flying V Bar & Grill, a Southwestern-style casual eatery with a glowing fireplace and a view of the 18th hole of the Canyon Course.

ABOVE: *Southwestern cuisine is a favorite at this desert resort.*

AT A GLANCE: *371 rooms with whirlpool, private balcony/patio, mountain/city view; 27 suites with whirlpool, fireplace, private balcony/patio, mountain/city view, some with Jacuzzi. 5 restaurants, cooking courses, fitness center, spa, steam room, sauna, whirlpool, beauty salon, shops, supervised children's programs, outdoor (heated) pool, day/night tennis, golf, bicycling, hiking, nature walking.* NEARBY: *movie theaters, rollerblading, horseback riding, hot-air ballooning, skating.*

Grilled Swordfish Tacos with Citrus Salsa and Jicama Slaw

Marinade:
Zest of 1 orange, grated
Zest of 1 lime, grated
Juice of 1 orange

Fish:
12 (2-ounce) swordfish medallions
Salt and pepper to taste

Citrus Salsa:
2 Ruby Red grapefruits, peeled and
   sectioned
1 orange, peeled and sectioned
2 limes, peeled and sectioned
¼ small red onion, thinly sliced
1 jalapeño, seeded and diced
2 tablespoons chopped cilantro
½ teaspoon olive oil
Salt and pepper to taste

Jicama Slaw:
1 pound jicama (see note on page 45),
   julienned
Juice of 2 limes

3 tablespoons finely snipped chives
1 red bell pepper, seeded, julienned
Salt and pepper to taste

Tacos:
12 (6-inch) flour tortillas
24 limestone (Bibb) lettuce leaves
24 sprigs of cilantro
12 slices red tomato
12 slices yellow tomato

Prepare the marinade. Combine all the ingredients. Marinate the fish in the refrigerator for 60 minutes.

Prepare the citrus salsa. Toss all the ingredients.

Prepare the jicama slaw. Mix all the ingredients.

Prepare the fish. Remove from the marinade and place in a well-greased wire basket on a grill rack directly over medium coals. Season with salt and pepper and grill to taste or until it flakes when tested with a fork; turn once, halfway through grilling.

To assemble the tacos, heat the tortillas and fill with the lettuce, cilantro, fish, tomato, and citrus salsa

Yield: 6 servings (2 tacos per serving)

· · · · · · · · ·
BELOW: *Loews Ventana Canyon Resort has two PGA champion-ship courses.*

Rancho de los Caballeros

Rancho de los Caballeros, an hour's drive from Phoenix, has been welcoming visitors since 1947. This property sets the standard for ranch resorts in America.

Wickenburg, Arizona

(800) 684-5030 or (520) 684-5484

$$

golf

Reminiscent of the Old West in charm and hospitality — but with all the modern comforts — the ranch offers riding on more than twenty thousand acres of rolling hills and flowering desert. A corral of 90 horses managed by seasoned cowboys caters to all levels of riding ability.

Golf on the Los Caballeros course is the second most popular activity for guests. The 18-hole championship course is ranked fifth in the state by *Golf Digest* and offers some of the most challenging play in Arizona. Here, coyotes and jackrabbits cross your path and breathtaking vistas distract you from your game.

Cookout rides, family rides, desert jeep tours, trap and skeet shooting, and nature hikes all entice guests into the surrounding desert. A children's program for ages 5 – 12 offers riding, exploring, games, and arts and crafts.

For a closer look at the wildlife of the region, many visitors choose to saddle up and take a guided ride. The residents of the Sonoran Desert — owls, coyotes, and javalinas — can be glimpsed sometimes, but it's a sure bet riders will get to enjoy the beauty of this region, including its many species of cactus. Regal saguaro cacti are seen silhouetted against the sky, and often the cactus wren can be spotted nearby.

In the festive Southwestern-style dining room, chef Dan Martin has been serving dishes using local fare for the past two decades, and Mary Jane Almand has been preparing baked goods at Rancho de los Caballeros even longer. One night a week, the resort arranges a cookout under the stars, featuring steaks, ribs, and chicken grilled over a mesquite fire.

ABOVE: This resort is a golfer's paradise as well as a dude ranch.

AT A GLANCE: *46 rooms with private patio, scenic view; 23 suites with Jacuzzi, fireplace. Restaurant, supervised children's programs, outdoor (heated) pool, tennis, golf, bicycling, hiking, nature walking, horseback riding, hot-air ballooning.* NEARBY: *shops, movie theaters, watersports, boating, marina, fishing.*

Roasted Pepper and Corn Soup

1 red bell pepper
1 green bell pepper
1 medium onion, diced
½ cup diced green chili
1 tablespoon minced garlic
Olive oil
1 cup butter, melted
1 cup all-purpose flour
1 quart milk or light cream
2 cups fresh corn kernels, or frozen,
    thawed
Salt and white pepper to taste
1 cup canola oil
2 large corn tortillas, julienned

Roast the bell peppers. Place under a broiler or hold over a gas burner until charred, steam in a sealed plastic bag for 10 minutes (to facilitate peeling), then peel and seed.

Purée in a blender or food processor, adding a little water if necessary to make a smooth paste.

Sauté the onion, chili, and garlic in the olive oil.

Mix the butter and flour over low heat to make a roux. Bring the milk to a boil in a heavy saucepan, then add the roux to thicken it. Let simmer. Add the sautéed onion mixture, pepper purée, and corn. Season with the salt and pepper and simmer for 30 minutes.

Heat the canola oil and fry the tortillas. Serve these as a garnish for the soup.

Yield: 4 – 6 servings

BELOW: *Colorful Rancho de los Caballeros has been welcoming visitors for half a century.*

Gaston's White River Resort

Gaston's is an Arkansas institution. Begun in 1958 with 20 acres along the White River, it comprised six small cottages and six boats — and the makings of some of America's best fishing for rainbow and brown trout.

Lakeview, Arkansas

(870) 431-5202

$

fishing

Forty years later, the Ozark resort spans a vast three hundred acres and attracts serious fishermen from all over North America. It has witnessed many changes, but fortunately for the generations of vacationers who come to this riverside retreat — many of them the children and grandchildren of Al Gaston's original patrons — it has maintained its unique traditions, even improving upon some of them.

Today, the resort is owned and operated by Al's son, Jim, and his wife, Jill. The friendly couple help beginners learn the art of trout fishing and offer advanced fishermen instruction in the finer points of fly fishing by providing professional assistance from visiting experts.

Gaston's restaurant, which sits on the banks of the White River, offers a taste of the river's rich bounty. It also serves steaks and seafood, accompanied by a selection of fine wines.

ABOVE: For 40 years this friendly resort has been a mecca for rainbow and brown trout fishing.

AT A GLANCE: *74 cottages and 6 suites, all with fireplace, private balcony/patio, river/mountain view. Restaurant, shops, supervised children's programs, outdoor pool, tennis, bicycling, rollerblading, hiking, nature walking, boating, marina, fishing.* NEARBY: *beauty salon, movie theaters, antique shops, golf, horseback riding, scuba diving, snorkeling, windsurfing, river rafting, Bull Shoals State Park, Bull Shoals Lake, trout fishing, fly fishing school.*

Trout Supreme

3 tablespoons chopped green onion,
  with tops
4 tablespoons butter or margarine
½ cup Chablis
1½ cups whipping cream
6 egg yolks, beaten
1 teaspoon seasoned salt
1 cup cooked crabmeat
6 trout fillets

In a heavy saucepan, simmer the onion in some of the butter for 3 minutes. Add the Chablis and the cream and simmer for 10 minutes. Bring to a boil, then remove from heat. Add the egg yolks and the salt and mix. Add the crabmeat and mix again.

Preheat the oven to 400°F. Place the trout skin side down in a baking pan. Brush with butter and bake for 10 – 15 minutes or until flaky. Cover with the sauce and return to the oven for an additional 1 – 2 minutes. Serve immediately.

Yield: 6 servings

· · · · · · · · · · ·
BELOW: *Seafood, steaks, and lots of spokes please diners at Gaston's White River Resort.*

La Costa Resort and Spa

*W*hether you seek activity or relaxation, challenging courses or soothing treatments, you'll find it all at La Costa. You can even take your work on vacation with you — every room has a fax machine.

Carlsbad, California

*(800) 854-5000 or
(760) 931-7591*

$$ – $$$$

golf / spa / tennis

This internationally known resort located 30 miles north of San Diego draws visitors for its golf and tennis facilities as well as its separate men's and women's health spas.

La Costa has a golf school and two championship courses that are home to the annual Mercedes Championships, the PGA Tour's invitational event featuring the reigning champions from the previous year's PGA and Senior PGA tour events. The North Course is hilly with plenty of sand, while the South Course challenges players with a prevailing wind off the Pacific Ocean.

For those who'd rather pick up a racquet, La Costa has tennis clinics and 21 courts, in grass, clay, and California composite hard surfaces. A favorite with serious players, the courts have hosted the Davis Cup and annually host the Toshiba Tennis Classic, a prelude on the women's tour to the U.S. Open Championships.

La Costa massages include Swedish, shiatsu, reflexology, aromatherapy, and reike. Skin care ranges from aromatherapy with natural essential oils to hydrating paraffin treatment for seriously dehydrated skin. To soothe those tired muscles, visitors can enjoy an herbal wrap — the entire body is enveloped in warm, herb-saturated linen sheets — or relax with water therapy using minerals specially chosen to ease stiff joints or to improve circulation.

Five restaurants complete the resort experience. Three nights a week, Pisces, the signature restaurant of La Costa, delights diners with gourmet seafood. Ristorante Figaro offers Italian cuisine in a classically European dining room. Pasta, veal, and chicken specialties are accompanied by wines from an extensive selection featuring Italian, French, and California labels. Other choices include Brasserie La Costa for informal al fresco eating and the Center Court Restaurant for indoor and outdoor dining at the stadium tennis court.

ABOVE: *Tennis, anyone? This California resort features a grand total of 21 courts.*

AT A GLANCE: *396 rooms and 77 suites, many with private balcony / patio, some with golf course view; 5 houses. 5 restaurants, fitness center, spa, steam room, sauna, whirlpool, beauty salon, shops, outdoor (heated) pools, day / night tennis, golf.* NEARBY: *movie theaters, bicycling, rollerblading, hiking, nature walking, horseback riding, hot-air ballooning, beach, scuba diving, snorkeling, windsurfing, boating, marina, fishing.*

Tuna Tartare with Crème Fraîche and Beluga Caviar

12 ounces fresh yellowfin tuna,
   diced ½ inch

1 tablespoon soy sauce

½ teaspoon powdered wasabi (see
   note), mixed with 2 tablespoons
   water

1 teaspoon chopped cilantro

1 teaspoon snipped chives

Salt and pepper to taste

4 quail eggs (available in specialty food
   shops)

1 cup crème fraîche or sour cream

2 ounces beluga caviar

1 cup chervil sprigs

½ cup sun-dried tomato oil
   (optional)

In a bowl, mix well the tuna, soy sauce, wasabi mixed with water, cilantro, chives, and salt and pepper.

In a non-stick pan, cook the quail eggs sunny side up for about 3 minutes.

Place a 3½-inch ring mold in the center of a serving plate and fill it, almost to the rim, with the tuna mixture. Spread the crème fraîche on top and remove the ring. Top with the caviar, quail eggs, and 1 sprig of chervil. Garnish the plate with the remaining sprigs of chervil and the tomato oil, if desired.

Note: Wasabi, also known as Japanese horseradish, is available, in both powdered and paste form, in Asian markets or specialty food shops.

Yield: 4 appetizer servings

LEFT: *La Costa has two complete spas: one for women and one for men.*

Quail Lodge Resort and Golf Club

Quail Lodge Resort and Golf Club blends into its natural setting so well that it is home not just to guests seeking a getaway but also to wildlife and waterfowl. Ducks quack contentedly in the 10 small lakes that dot the grounds of this resort.

Carmel, California

(800) 538-9516

$$ – $$$$

golf

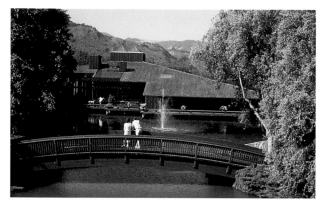

The lakes, hills, and oak-shaded lawns of Quail Lodge, located on 850 acres in Carmel Valley, help complete the picture: a casually elegant resort where activity and relaxation go hand in hand.

Perhaps best known for its golf facilities — an 18-hole championship course, two practice putting greens, and a seven-acre practice range — the resort also offers plenty of activities off the links. Guests can revel in the natural setting with a picnic lunch, a bike ride, a horseback ride, or a deep-sea fishing excursion along the Monterey Peninsula. Available as well are hot-air balloon rides and winery tours.

Whatever your preferred activities, a highlight of this resort is the Covey Restaurant, which overlooks a curving footbridge in the beautiful setting that makes Quail Lodge a glorious retreat for both human and animal life.

Chef Bob Williamson, trained in Switzerland and London, begins meal preparations by selecting herbs from his courtyard herb garden. Williamson's penchant for serving European dishes with an American accent have earned the Covey Restaurant many accolades. Menu offerings start with such appetizers as Russian caviar or Burgundy escargots. The main course might be sautéed sweetbreads, black currant duck, or an innovative dish chosen from the spa cuisine. The meal closes with a sweet such as raspberries Chambord or crème brûlée.

Upon check-in, every guest is greeted with a bottle of Quail Lodge Chardonnay.

ABOVE: *Lakes, hills, and oak-shaded lawns combine to create a resort where activity and relaxation go hand in hand.*

AT A GLANCE: *86 rooms with private balcony/patio, garden/golf course view; 14 suites with hot tub, fireplace, private balcony/patio, garden/golf course view; 4 villas with hot tub. 2 restaurants, outdoor (heated) pool, tennis, golf, bicycling, nature walking.* NEARBY: *cooking courses, fitness center, spa, steam room, sauna, whirlpool, beauty salon, shops, movie theaters, day/night tennis, rollerblading, hiking, horseback riding, hot-air ballooning, beach, scuba diving, boating, marina, fishing.*

Scallops with Champagne Sauce

Champagne Sauce:
¾ cup Champagne or Riesling
1 shallot, finely chopped
¾ cup clam juice
½ cup whipping cream
1 tablespoon flour
2 tablespoons soft butter
Pinch of white pepper

Scallops:
1½ pounds large fresh scallops
Salt and pepper
All-purpose flour to dust
Melted butter

Prepare the Champagne sauce. In a heavy saucepan, rapidly boil the Champagne and chopped shallot for 2 minutes. Add the clam juice and reduce the mixture to about ¾ cup. Add the cream and bring to a boil. Mix the flour and the butter to make a roux, then whisk this into the sauce. Reduce the heat so that the sauce does not boil and maintains a consistency of light cream. If the sauce is too thin, add a little more of the flour and butter mixture; if it is too thick, add more of the cream or clam juice. Season with the pepper.

Prepare the scallops. Lightly season with salt and pepper. Dust with the flour. Place on a broiling pan and brush with the butter. Broil for 2 – 3 minutes, ensuring that the scallops do not brown.

Strain the Champagne sauce over the scallops and serve hot.

Yield: 4 servings

Nasturtium Salad

1 teaspoon Dijon mustard
2 teaspoons Champagne vinegar
3 tablespoons olive oil
Salt and pepper to taste
6 – 8 ounces mixed greens
2 – 3 ounces edible nasturtium leaves
  and flowers (see note)

Vigorously whisk the mustard, vinegar, oil, and salt and pepper until well blended. Add the greens and the nasturtium leaves and flowers and toss.

Note: Edible, peppery-flavored nasturtium leaves and flowers are available in specialty produce markets or supermarkets that carry gourmet produce. Flowers bought from a florist have been sprayed with pesticides and are not to be eaten.

Yield: 4 servings

ABOVE: *Ducks fill the many lakes that dot the grounds of Quail Lodge.*

La Quinta Resort & Club

Whether they swing a golf club or a tennis racquet, guests of this resort located near the Santa Rosa Mountains southeast of Palm Springs place it at the top of their list.

La Quinta, California

(800) 598-3828 or (760) 564-4111

$$ – $$$

golf/tennis

La Quinta dates back to the days of Hollywood glamor, when stars like Greta Garbo, Ginger Rogers, Clark Gable, and Katherine Hepburn were frequent guests. During the filming of *Jezebel,* a certain Bette Davis took a break from the set, boldly declaring, "I'm going to La Quinta." Since 1926, this classic resort featuring Spanish-style casita accommodations and twice-daily maid service has served as an oasis for those who like to play and be pampered.

Set amid swaying palms on 45 acres of orange, lemon, and grapefruit trees, La Quinta Resort & Club is the perfect place to do as much — or as little — as you choose.

For active vacationers, golf is a top attraction. There are four choices: the PGAWEST™ TPC® Stadium Golf Course, the Jack Nicklaus Tournament Course, and La Quinta Resort's Mountain and Dunes courses. For those who'd rather take a swing at a slightly larger ball, the La Quinta Tennis Club has 30 courts with Har-Tru clay, grass, and hard surfaces. And if all that physical exercise makes for some stiff and tired muscles, La Quinta features 38 whirlpools and 25 swimming pools to soothe away the aches.

Dining ranks as a top activity at this posh resort. Montañas Restaurant, located in an original 1926 adobe structure, serves fish and seafood creations such as swordfish in Cioppino broth, Provençale tiger shrimps, and red snapper en papillote, as well as poultry, beef, and lamb dishes. Morgans Restaurant, named for the resort's founder, Walter Morgan, features a wide array of innovative American dishes. Other La Quinta Resort dining spots include a restaurant featuring regional Mexican cuisine, a bistro, and, for the more health conscious, the tennis clubhouse.

La Quinta Resort is noted for its attentive service — it makes every guest feel like a celebrity. And if the comfortable surroundings inspire you to greatness, you'll be in fine company. It was here that Irving Berlin wrote "White Christmas" and Frank Capra turned a short story into the screenplay for *It Happened One Night.*

ABOVE: *Located near Palm Springs, this resort recalls the days of Hollywood glamor.*

AT A GLANCE: *640 rooms, some with fireplace, private balcony/patio, mountain view; 27 suites, some with Jacuzzi, fireplace, private balcony/patio, mountain view. 5 restaurants, cooking courses, fitness center, spa, whirlpool, beauty salon, shops, supervised children's programs, outdoor (heated) pool, day/night tennis, golf, bicycling.* NEARBY: *hiking, nature walking, horseback riding, hot-air ballooning.*

Morgans Braised Lamb Shanks

This secret recipe from Morgans Restaurant at La Quinta Resort comes with a recommendation that it be served with fresh asparagus and garlic mashed potatoes or mushroom risotto.

6 lamb shanks, Frenched (see note)
Salt and pepper to taste
¼ cup olive oil
6 garlic cloves
2 cups diced carrot, celery, and onion
½ cup tomato paste
1 sprig of rosemary
2 sprigs of thyme
1¼ cups dry red wine
2 quarts beef stock

Season the lamb with salt and pepper.

Heat the oil in a large roasting pan with a lid. Brown the lamb on all sides, then remove from the pan.

Cook the garlic and diced vegetables in the pan until the vegetables are tender. Add the tomato paste, rosemary, thyme, and wine. Reduce the wine by half. Add the stock.

Return the lamb to the pan and simmer, covered, for 1½ – 2 hours or until tender.

Note: A Frenched lamb shank has the meat cut away from the end of the chop to expose part of the bone.

Yield: 6 servings

· · · · · · · · · ·

BELOW: *Morgans braised lamb is a favorite with La Quinta diners.*

The Oaks at Ojai

The Oaks at Ojai welcomes people of all fitness levels and all ages, catering to those who don't necessarily try to look like supermodels or top athletes.

Ojai, California

(800) 753-OAKS

$

spa

This Ojai Valley resort, just a 90-minute drive from Los Angeles, is a getaway for those people who want to both feel and look their very best. It's the perfect place for not only fitness buffs but anyone seeking a stress-free break from the realities of everyday life.

The Oaks features a thousand-calorie-per-day menu, but any guest who's still hungry can ask for "athlete" portions. All meals are made with only fresh fruits and vegetables, seafood, poultry, and seasonings, as well as whole grains.

But prudent dining is just part of the total experience at The Oaks at Ojai. Guests are pampered with an array of treatments: facials, body scrubs, massages, manicures, pedicures, and paraffin treatments, all available on an à la carte basis. They also participate in daily classes — stretching, aerobic, and resistance — choosing from among the 16 low-stress classes that are offered every day. Fashion, medical, and motivational seminars are popular draws as well.

To owner Sheila Cluff, a grandmother, The Oaks is more than a business — it's her home. This fitness expert, who also owns The Palms at Palm Springs, is the author of four fitness books and a spa cookbook.

ABOVE: The Oaks at Ojai features a low-calorie menu.

AT A GLANCE: *44 rooms; 2 triple cottages. Restaurant, cooking courses, fitness center, spa, sauna, whirlpool, beauty salon, shops, outdoor (heated) pool, rollerblading, hiking, nature walking.* NEARBY: *movie theaters, day/night tennis, golf, bicycling, horseback riding, beach, boating, marina, fishing, jeep tours.*

Cheese-Stuffed Zucchini

3 (6-inch) zucchini
½ cup low-fat creamed cottage
  cheese
2½ tablespoons grated Parmesan
  cheese
1 tablespoon chopped scallion
1 tablespoon minced parsley

Preheat the oven to 350°F.

Steam the zucchini for 2 minutes (or place in a plastic bag and microwave for 2 minutes). Cool. Halve lengthwise and scoop out the seeds.

Combine the cottage cheese, 1½ tablespoons of the Parmesan cheese, the scallion, and the parsley. Mix well. Spoon into the zucchini shells.

Sprinkle with the remaining tablespoon of Parmesan cheese and bake until the zucchini is heated through and the cheese is melted and browned.

Yield: 6 servings

. . . .
BELOW: *Resort owner Sheila Cluff (second from left), a fitness expert and author, leads guests on a morning walk.*

The Palms at Palm Springs

You may have heard the expression "No pain, no gain." Well, the message at The Palms at Palm Springs is "No fun, no gain." Set in scenic Palm Springs, this spa keeps visitors smiling and well fed.

Palm Springs, California

(800) 753-PALM

$

spa

A typical day at The Palms begins with a walk, which can vary from an easy stroll, for beginners, to a demanding hike, for guests at an advanced level of fitness. After a breakfast of fresh fruit, muffins, beverage, and a vitamin pack, vacationers participate in a body awareness class, where they stretch to warm up their muscles in preparation for a more strenuous workout.

"The Palms is for the spa-goer who seeks more than just a spa experience," explains Bruce Taylor, the general manager. "Guests can be as rigorous as they wish — they can play it by ear and see how they feel." Workouts vary according to fitness level and interest. The range of choices includes aqua aerobics, aquatoning, creative aerobics, and body dynamics.

After the morning class, guests take lunch at poolside, then select another class, perhaps adding some weight training or a step class. Finally, it's time to wind down with yoga or some other form of relaxation.

In keeping with the fitness theme, dinners at The Palms are health-conscious, showcasing dishes from recipes that owner Sheila Cluff has refined during her many years in the fitness business.

ABOVE: Set in scenic Palm Springs, this spa keeps visitors busy, smiling, and well fed.

AT A GLANCE: *33 rooms, some with private patio. Restaurant, cooking courses, fitness center, spa, sauna, whirlpool, beauty salon, shops, outdoor (heated) pool, hiking, nature walking.* NEARBY: *movie theaters, day / night tennis, golf, bicycling, rollerblading, horseback riding, hot-air ballooning, cross-country skiing, street fair.*

Childrens Mem Hosp
For deposit only

Dr

Oriental Rice Salad

2 cups cooked brown rice
1 cup sliced mushrooms
1 cup snow peas or edible pea pods
1 cup thinly sliced celery (cut
    diagonally)
½ cup slivered red bell pepper
½ cup minced scallion
1 tablespoon sesame oil
¼ cup rice vinegar
2 tablespoons low-sodium soy sauce
¼ cup toasted slivered almonds

Combine the rice, mushrooms, snow peas, celery, bell pepper, and scallion. Toss lightly.

Mix well the oil, vinegar, and soy sauce.

Toss the rice mixture with the dressing and the almonds. Serve chilled.

Yield: 8 servings

Lemon Chicken

1 pound skinless, boneless chicken
    breast, cut into 1 x ¼-inch pieces
2 tablespoons lemon juice
1 egg
1 teaspoon arrowroot
2 cups mushrooms, cut the size of the
    chicken pieces
2 cups cooked brown rice, heated
6 lemon verbena leaves, or lemon slices
    and parsley sprigs

Sprinkle the chicken with the lemon juice. Cover and refrigerate for 30 minutes, then steam for 10 minutes or until tender and opaque.

Drain the juices from the cooked chicken into a measuring cup: there should be ½ cup; if necessary, add water to make up the difference. Put in a saucepan with the egg and the arrowroot and cook over low heat, stirring, until thickened. Add the chicken and mushrooms and heat through.

Serve over the brown rice, garnished with the lemon verbena leaves.

Yield: 6 servings

. . . .
BELOW: *A typical day at The Palms begins with an exhilarating walk.*

Loews Coronado Bay Resort

Located at the tip of a private peninsula off Coronado Island, Loews Coronado Bay Resort offers the relaxed atmosphere of a seaside resort and the easy access of a city getaway.

*San Diego,
California*

(800) 81-LOEWS

$$

beach

Situated just minutes from San Diego, it transports guests into an environment as serene as the world of the gulls that slowly ride the sea breezes overhead.

Although there's a beach nearby, this resort is not a true beach getaway but a sumptuous seaside resort. Water recreation abounds, from sailing in San Diego Bay to wave-running and kayaking. Landlubbers will also find plenty to do, with access to beach cruisers, mountain and tandem bikes, and miles of paths and trails to ride or hike into stylish Coronado. Tennis lovers can brush up on their game by taking advantage of the professional instruction offered on five bayside courts.

The focal point of the complex is its extensive marina, where vessels from the seven seas have resort privileges such as one-of-a-kind "room service" right on their own yachts. Loews Coronado Bay guests can treat themselves to a taste of the maritime life with a sail or a cruise from the docks.

All this activity can work up an appetite. Dining is considered one of the most important pastimes at Loews Coronado Bay Resort, recipient of such accolades as *San Diego* magazine's Best Hotel/Resort Dining award. Much of this attention is due to the talents of executive chef James Boyce, who oversees all preparation, from the growing of the herbs (check out the garden during complimentary tours every Thursday) to the presentation of the meals. The Azzura Point restaurant, which features views of the city and the bay, uses fresh Pacific seafood in a Mediterranean-inspired cuisine. Entrées might include herb-roasted rack of lamb with curried vegetables, roasted Black Sea bass atop a ratatouille of artichoke, fennel, and sun-dried tomatoes, or roasted breast of capon with potatoes, tomatoes, olives, and rosemary dressing.

ABOVE: Water recreation abounds, from sailing in San Diego Bay to wave-running and kayaking.

AT A GLANCE: *406 rooms and 25 suites, all with private balcony, ocean view; 4 villas with Jacuzzi, private balcony, ocean view; 3 suites with Jacuzzi, fireplace, private balcony, ocean view. 3 restaurants, cooking courses, fitness center, spa, steam room, sauna, whirlpool, beauty salon, shops, supervised children's programs, outdoor (heated) pool, day/night tennis, bicycling, rollerblading, nature walking, beach, windsurfing, boating, marina.* NEARBY: *movie theaters, golf, hiking, horseback riding, hot-air ballooning, scuba diving, snorkeling, fishing.*

Rock Shrimp with Mediterranean-Style Bow-Tie Pasta

Salt and pepper

1 pound broccoli florets, split into small pieces (8 cups)

2 slices Canadian bacon, diced ¼ inch

3 tablespoons olive oil

12 ounces bow-tie pasta

1 pound Pacific rock shrimp, cleaned

3 garlic cloves, chopped

1 small jalapeño, seeded and finely chopped

⅓ cup finely chopped onion

1 small sprig of rosemary, finely chopped

2 tablespoons tiny French capers, drained

2 tablespoons diced sun-dried tomatoes

4 tablespoons sliced kalamata olives

½ cup plum tomatoes, seeded and diced ¼ inch

1 small sprig of marjoram, finely chopped

1 small sprig of oregano, finely chopped

Bring to a boil 2 quarts of water with 1 tablespoon of salt and 1 tablespoon of pepper. Add the broccoli and boil for 2 – 3 minutes. Drain, cool under water, then drain again.

Fry the bacon over medium heat until crisp and slightly browned. Remove with a slotted spoon and place on paper towels.

Bring to a boil over high heat 4 quarts of water with 1 tablespoon of salt and ½ tablespoon of the oil. Add the pasta and boil for 10 minutes. Drain thoroughly.

Meanwhile, heat 2 tablespoons of the oil in a large sauté pan over high heat. Season the shrimp with salt and pepper and sauté for 1 minute. Add the garlic, jalapeño, onion, and rosemary and cook for 1 minute. Add the capers, sun-dried tomatoes, 2 tablespoons of the olives, diced tomato, and cooked broccoli. Cook, stirring, for 2 – 3 minutes. Season to taste with the marjoram and oregano.

Toss the pasta with the shrimp mixture, remaining ½ tablespoon of oil, and remaining 2 tablespoons of olives. Serve in a large pasta dish.

Yield: 6 servings

. . . .

ABOVE: *Rock shrimp with Mediterranean-style bow-tie pasta is a favorite dish of James Boyce, executive chef at Loews Coronado Bay Resort.*

Rancho Bernardo Inn

E ven the most dedicated golfer would be satisfied with 126 holes — which makes Rancho Bernardo Inn a hole-in-one for anyone seeking a golf vacation. With 45 holes on the premises and direct access to additional courses, this is a dream come true for link lovers.

San Diego, California

(800) 770-7530 or (619) 675-8500

$$

golf

Guests can choose between an 18-hole championship course and a 27-hole course, which together feature some 60 bunkers and such challenges as lakes, waterfalls, and clumps of olive and eucalyptus trees. Four additional courses located just off the premises include protected wildlife habitats and granite rocks that still bear the markings of the Pechanga Indians. For those eager to take a few strokes off their play, the Golf University offers techniques inspired by its founder, the avid golfer Ken Blanchard, co-author of *The One-Minute Manager*.

Off the fairways, the inn offers a complete spa and fitness center with a full range of workout equipment. Shiatsu and Swedish masseurs work out the kinks.

El Bizcocho is Rancho Bernardo Inn's signature restaurant. "El Biz" overlooks the golf course and the San Pasqual Mountains, but these views must compete with classical French fare and a wine list of more than 550 labels. Appetizers include such dishes as Maine lobster with toasted Roma tomatoes, avocado, and fresh horseradish, or smoked salmon with onions, capers, and parsley, followed by brioche and lobster bisque with Armagnac. Entrées are apt to change with the season, but specialties such as roasted Long Island duckling, sautéed veal loin, and grilled Norwegian salmon with portabella mushrooms, fresh basil, tomato, and vermouth sauce are likely to make an appearance at any time.

The restaurant is favored by local residents and visitors alike for its Sunday Champagne Brunch, featuring an omelet station, seafood entrées, and, from the dessert bar, bread pudding borrowed from a recipe by actor Vincent Price (see recipe opposite).

ABOVE: *The comfortable rooms feature a hint of the Southwest.*

AT A GLANCE: *285 rooms with private balcony/patio, mountain/golf course view; 58 suites with private balcony/patio, mountain/golf course view, 2 with Jacuzzi, fireplace. 2 restaurants, fitness center, spa, steam room, sauna, whirlpool, shops, supervised children's programs, outdoor (heated) pool, day/night tennis, golf, bicycling, rollerblading, hiking, nature walking. NEARBY: cooking courses, beauty salon, movie theaters, indoor pool, indoor tennis, horseback riding, hot-air ballooning, beach, scuba diving, snorkeling, windsurfing, boating, marina, river rafting, fishing, hunting, skating.*

Vincent Price's Bread Pudding with Crème Anglaise

Bread Pudding:
3 tablespoons butter
¾ cup brown sugar
½ cup raisins
12 slices white bread
4 eggs, beaten
4 cups milk
1½ teaspoons vanilla

Crème Anglaise (yields 3 cups):
6 egg yolks
¾ cup sugar
2 cups milk
Pinch of salt
Vanilla to taste

Prepare the pudding. Preheat the oven to 350°F.

Use the butter to grease an 8 x 12-inch glass baking dish. Sprinkle the sugar and raisins evenly over the butter. Line the dish with the bread slices. Mix the egg, milk, and vanilla. Pour this over the bread. Place the dish in a shallow pan of warm water and bake, uncovered, for 75 minutes.

Meanwhile, prepare the crème anglaise. Beat the egg yolks and sugar until smooth. Bring the milk to a boil. Add the salt and vanilla. Very gradually combine the egg mixture with the hot milk. Boil for just 1 second. Strain and cool to room temperature before serving.

Serve the pudding hot, with the crème anglaise.

Yield: 8 servings

• • • • • • • • • •
BELOW: *Rancho Bernardo is favored for its golf facilities.*

The Broadmoor

Visitors to Colorado tend to expect Rocky Mountain ruggedness in their accommodations, but this resort could compete with any New York five-star hotel.

Colorado Springs, Colorado

(800) 633-7711

$$ – $$$

golf / spa / tennis

Lit by a crystal chandelier, fitted with Oriental rugs, decorated with fine art: this is The Broadmoor, one of the smartest resorts in the West.

The posh three-thousand-acre resort opened its doors in 1918, immediately attracting numerous celebrities. Its New York architects brought to Colorado Springs an Old World grandeur, with their Italian Renaissance stucco buildings, Toulouse-Lautrec lithographs, a collection of 17th-century art, and works dating back to the Ming and Tsing dynasties.

Guests of The Broadmoor have included visiting royalty, prominent politicians, a string of movie stars, and no fewer than six U.S. presidents. Today the cachet of the resort still attracts famous names, but it is also favored by the less rich and powerful — people who simply want to get away for a weekend of relaxation and pampering.

The sumptuousness of The Broadmoor is evident throughout the grounds and in the guest rooms. The mythical horses of a two-hundred-year-old fountain imported from Italy in 1923 continue to stand guard, and each room is decorated with original works of art.

The $16-million golf, tennis, and spa facility offers massage, aromatherapy, hydrotherapy, and other treatments, ranging from mud wraps to salt glow. Three championship golf courses and tennis activities directed by Hall of Famer Dennis Ralston keep sports lovers active.

Meals here can be as healthful or as sinful as you please. All restaurants include Cuisine Vivante — low-fat, high-protein — selections on their menus. The formal Penrose Room serves international cuisine, while Charles Court features award-winning wines with its meals and the Lake Terrace Dining Room is known for its Sunday brunch. The Tavern and Garden Room is a steak and chop house, the golf club includes two restaurants with a country club atmosphere, Spensers offers a view of the city and the Rocky Mountains, and Julie's is open all day for light eating.

AT A GLANCE: *608 rooms and 92 suites, all with fireplace, private balcony / patio, scenic view. 9 restaurants, cooking courses, fitness center, spa, steam room, sauna, whirlpool, beauty salon, shops, movie theaters, supervised children's programs, indoor / outdoor (heated) pool, indoor / outdoor / night tennis, golf, bicycling, sleigh rides.* NEARBY: *rollerblading, hiking, nature walking, horseback riding, hot-air ballooning, river rafting, fishing, hunting, downhill / cross-country skiing, snowboarding, skating, snowshoeing, snowmobiling.*

ABOVE: *The Broadmoor is the epitome of elegance.*

Chicken with Wild Mushrooms

4 (8-ounce) skinless, boneless chicken
   breasts
Salt and pepper to taste
2 tablespoons butter
8 ounces mixed wild mushrooms
1 shallot, finely chopped
1 garlic clove, finely chopped
2 tablespoons Madeira
2 tablespoons herbes de Provence
2 cups chicken stock

Preheat the oven to 400°F. Grease a baking pan with a wire rack.

Flatten the chicken with a mallet and season with salt and pepper on both sides.

Brown half of the butter slightly in a hot pan. Add the mushrooms, shallot, garlic, and salt and pepper. Cook for 2 minutes, then deglaze with the Madeira. Add the herbes de Provence and simmer for 2 minutes. Allow to cool, then place in the center of each chicken breast. Roll the breast and lay it on a piece of plastic wrap. Roll the wrap very tightly so that it resembles a sausage. Cover with aluminum foil and bake in the prepared pan for 15 – 20 minutes.

Meanwhile, reduce the chicken stock by half. Remove the chicken from the oven and add its cooking juices to the reduced stock. Adjust the seasoning. Whisk the remainder of the butter and spread it over the chicken. Serve hot.

Yield: 4 servings

ABOVE: *The Broad-moor's nine restaurants serve meals both deliciously sensible and indulgently rich.*

Keystone Resort

Beautiful mountain scenery, breathtaking ski runs, and relaxing après-ski activities are to be expected at this Colorado resort. What surprises many is Keystone's emphasis on fine dining — and cooking.

Keystone, Colorado

(800) 468-5004

$$ – $$$

mountain

The Keystone Cooking School, a three-day program (limited to 12 participants) that runs from Thursday through Sunday in the spring and fall months, is popular with people who want to learn from the masters. This culinary adventure is every bit as exciting as the downhill runs for which the resort is best known, and just as fulfilling as mastering the art of parallel skiing.

The cooking course begins when the manuals and chef uniforms are distributed at a Thursday reception. On Friday, class commences with a Continental breakfast followed by a morning lesson in cooking and culinary skills. No course is complete without a little free time, so class is dismissed in the afternoon to let students pursue Keystone's many pleasures — from mountain biking and golf in the spring and summer months to downhill or cross-country skiing, ice skating on Keystone Lake, and riding in a horse-drawn sleigh in the winter months.

If all that activity works up an appetite, students are in luck: early evening classes are followed by dinner with the chefs, which is served by the resort's banquet staff. On Saturday night the group enjoys a graduation dinner at the historic Ski Tip Lodge, which in the 1880s served as a stagecoach stop.

Guests who are reluctant to spend three days honing their culinary skills might consider the Cooking Class, held every Thursday evening. Participants can help cook that night's gourmet meal, which might range from Asian to Colorado to Cajun cuisine, then wine and dine with chef Bob Burden on the fruits of their labor.

Keystone is home to the Colorado Mountain College Culinary Institute, so it's no wonder that this Colorado wonderland is a dream come true for chefs as well as budding gourmets.

ABOVE: The Keystone Resort keeps vacationers active year round with activities ranging from snowshoeing to sailing.

AT A GLANCE: *255 rooms and 15 suites, many with private balcony / patio, mountain view; 746 other units (condos, houses, bed & breakfast accommodations), many with hot tub, fireplace, mountain view. 13 restaurants, cooking courses, fitness center, spa, steam room, sauna, whirlpool / Jacuzzi, shops, supervised children's programs, indoor / outdoor (heated) pool, indoor / outdoor tennis, golf, bicycling, rollerblading, hiking, nature walking, horseback riding, watersports, windsurfing, boating, marina, fishing, downhill / cross-country skiing, snowboarding, skating, snowshoeing, sleigh rides.* NEARBY: *beauty salon, movie theaters, hot-air ballooning, river rafting, hunting, snowmobiling, dogsledding.*

Corn Chutney

2 tablespoons butter

½ cup brown sugar

1 pound corn kernels (fresh or canned)

10 fresh tomatillos, halved (see note 1)

1 medium onion, finely diced

2 bunches green onions, finely chopped

2 garlic cloves, chopped

1 red bell pepper, seeded and finely chopped

2 poblanos, seeded and minced (see note 2)

1 tablespoon Red Molido chili powder

1 teaspoon chopped oregano

1 teaspoon salt

1 teaspoon black pepper

½ cup balsamic vinegar

Melt the butter and sugar in a saucepan. Stir. Mix in the corn, tomatillos, onion, green onion, garlic, bell pepper, poblano, chili powder, oregano, salt, and pepper. Cook thoroughly, while stirring. Add the vinegar. Continue to cook, stirring, until thickened.

Serve immediately with fish or chicken, or serve cold with chips or tortillas.

Note 1: Tomatillos, also known as Mexican green tomatoes, may be replaced with 8 – 10 cherry tomatoes, halved.

Note 2: Dark, sometimes black-green chilies ranging from mild to snappy, poblanos are available in Mexican markets and many supermarkets.

Yield: 6 cups (approximately)

Ski Tip Chocolate Cake

Cake:

1⅔ cups all-purpose flour

1 teaspoon baking powder

1 teaspoon baking soda

2½ tablespoons cocoa powder

10 tablespoons brown sugar

2½ tablespoons corn syrup

2 eggs

⅔ cup vegetable oil

1¼ cups milk

Frosting:

6 ounces sweet chocolate

2½ tablespoons whipping cream

Prepare the cake. Preheat the oven to 350°F. Grease and flour two 8-inch round cake pans.

Thoroughly blend all the ingredients using an electric mixer set at medium speed. Turn into the prepared pans and bake for 10 – 12 minutes or until the layer on the top rack springs back when lightly touched. Turn out on a wire rack to cool.

Meanwhile, make the frosting. Whisk the chocolate and cream in a double boiler until smooth. Cool to room temperature.

Frost the top of one layer, place the second layer on top, then frost the top.

Yield: 8 – 10 servings

BELOW: *Chef Chris Rybak welcomes diners to The Outpost.*

Vista Verde Ranch

T he term "western guest ranch" evokes images of saddles, trail rides, action-packed days, evenings around the campfire, and plenty of good food. Vista Verde Ranch offers all that — and more.

Steamboat Springs, Colorado

(800) 526-RIDE

$$

mountain

Guests at this upscale ranch, which spans more than five hundred wooded acres, find that their "bunkhouse" is a private log cabin tucked away in the mountains with antique furnishings and a crackling fire. Days can be spent horseback riding around alpine lakes and participating in the ranch rodeo, but at Vista Verde Ranch plenty of action is available off the saddle as well.

In the summer months, guests challenge themselves on mountain bikes, get a bird's-eye view of the mountain country from a hot-air balloon, or try their luck at fly fishing, backcountry hiking, or even white-water rafting on snow-fed rivers.

In the winter months, Vista Verde is blanketed with a heavy coat of powder. The horseback riding doesn't stop, but there are also sleigh rides and snowshoeing, dog-sledding, hot-air ballooning, and cross-country skiing on 19 miles of groomed trails.

Winter or summer, two factors are constant: nightly entertainment and wonderful eating. Fine dining is a feature of this guest ranch. A typical dinner menu might include Chateaubriand, Sicilian chicken with a generous portion of prosciutto and fresh basil, or blackened red snapper. All dishes come with a wine recommendation from the chef.

Vista Verde is a perfect getaway for anyone seeking an escape from the modern world. This ranch is proud to declare it has "only one telephone, a TV that is hard to find, a fax that is 25 miles away, and newspapers that are a day old."

ABOVE: *Guests of this upscale ranch stay in private log cabins set in the mountains.*

AT A GLANCE: *3 rooms with hot tub, private balcony, mountain view; 8 cabins with hot tub, fireplace, private patio, mountain view. Restaurant, cooking courses, fitness center, sauna, supervised children's programs, bicycling, hiking, nature walking, horseback riding, hot-air ballooning, rock climbing, hunting, fishing, river rafting, cross-country skiing, snowshoeing, dogsledding, sleigh rides. NEARBY: shops, movie theaters, outdoor (heated) pool, tennis, golf, beach, watersports, boating, downhill skiing, snowboarding, skating, snowmobiling.*

Granola

2 cups quick-cooking rolled oats
2 cups barley flakes
2 cups Grapenuts-brand cereal, or
  wheat flakes
1 cup bran flakes
1 cup sesame seeds
¾ cup sunflower oil
1 cup water
1 cup whole almonds
1 cup sun-dried cherries
1 cup sun-dried blueberries
1 cup raisins
½ cup honey
½ cup molasses
Fresh fruit
Yogurt

Preheat the oven to 350°F.

In a large bowl, mix the rolled oats, barley flakes, Grapenuts, bran flakes, sesame seeds, oil, and water. Bake in an ungreased 13 x 9-inch pan for 45 minutes, stirring every 15 minutes. Remove from the oven and cool, then stir in the almonds, cherries, blueberries, raisins, honey, and molasses.

Serve in cereal bowls with fresh fruit and yogurt.

Yield: 12 – 14 cups

Low-Fat Cocoa Brownies

½ cup unsweetened applesauce
¼ cup plus 2 tablespoons Dutch cocoa
  powder
2 tablespoons light corn syrup
1 cup sugar
¼ cup instant coffee
2 large egg whites
3 tablespoons non-fat sour cream
1 teaspoon vanilla
½ cup all-purpose flour

Preheat the oven to 350°F. Lightly oil an 8-inch square baking pan.

Combine the applesauce, cocoa, corn syrup, sugar, and coffee in a large mixing bowl. Stir with a wooden spoon until smooth. Stir in the egg whites, sour cream, and vanilla. Add the flour and stir just to incorporate. Turn into the prepared baking pan and bake for 18 minutes or until a cake tester inserted in the center comes out with a few moist crumbs clinging to it (the center of the brownie should be under-baked).

Cool in the pan on a wire rack for 30 minutes. To serve, cut into 2-inch squares.

Yield: 16 brownies

· · · · · · · · · · ·
BELOW: *Horseback riding across Vista Verde Ranch's vast expanses is popular in summertime.*

Vail Cascade Hotel and Club

T*he very mention of Vail brings to mind skis carving a trail down a powdery mountainside and sporty elegance in a spectacular alpine setting. Vail Cascade lives up to those images.*

Vail, Colorado

(800) 420-2424

$$$ – $$$$

mountain / spa

For more than a decade it has held the title of Vail's only AAA Four Diamond ski-in/ski-out hotel. At this resort, there's no need to hop a shuttle to the slopes: just 30 feet from the hotel, a $1-million quad chairlift whisks skiers to the top of Vail Mountain.

This resort may be set in the rugged Rockies, but its guests are treated to nothing but pure luxury. At check-in, a ski valet service takes your bulky ski equipment and keeps it until you're ready to hit the slopes. Each time you're set to go off again, the ski valet has your boots dry and warm.

The luxurious atmosphere pervades the resort, which recently underwent a $7-million facelift. The natural stone floors are adorned with handmade woolen area rugs, while a fireplace in the lobby invites guests to come over and warm up.

The Cascade Club keeps guests in top condition away from the slopes too. The official conditioning site for the U.S. ski team, the club has a complete weight room and offers plenty of competitive sports such as racquetball and squash. Daily aerobics and fitness classes are offered, as well as courses in yoga, martial arts, and self-defense. Spa treatments and beauty services are available.

When it comes time to relax, Alfredo's serves Northern Italian specialties with fine wines. For guests who prefer to carry the fitness theme over from the slopes and the Cascade Club, the Heart-Rate Café serves light and healthy pastas and salads, accompanied by a selection of juices.

AT A GLANCE: *289 rooms with private balcony / patio, scenic view; 28 suites with whirlpool / Jacuzzi / hot tub, private balcony / patio, scenic view; 63 (1 – 4-bedroom) condos. 3 restaurants, cooking courses, fitness center, spa, steam room, sauna, whirlpool, beauty salon, shops, movie theaters, supervised children's programs, outdoor (heated) pool, indoor / outdoor tennis, bicycling, rollerblading, nature walking, fishing, downhill skiing, snowboarding, snowshoeing.* NEARBY: *night tennis, golf, hiking, horseback riding, hot-air ballooning, watersports, river rafting, hunting, cross-country skiing, skating, snowmobiling, dogsledding, sleigh rides.*

ABOVE: *A quad chair-lift whisks visitors up the slopes.*

Crab Beignet

1½ cups all-purpose flour, sifted
2 cups water
¼ cup olive oil
⅛ teaspoon salt
⅛ teaspoon paprika
2 egg yolks
2 egg whites, stiffly beaten
5 ounces drained Dungeness crabmeat

Cream the flour, water, oil, salt, paprika, and egg yolks until smooth. Fold in the egg whites, then the crabmeat. Place a 2-ounce portion in a flan ring and fry in a sauté pan for 2 minutes. Turn and continue frying until golden brown.

Serve immediately.

Yield: 8 appetizer servings

Gorgonzola Bread Pudding

This bread pudding is excellent served as a side dish with rack of lamb.

1 tablespoon minced garlic
1 tablespoon chopped basil
2 cups whipping cream
1 teaspoon coarse kosher salt
1 teaspoon cracked black pepper
5 eggs, beaten
1 tablespoon chopped parsley
4 cups stale bread cubes
2 cups crumbled Gorgonzola cheese

Preheat the oven to 325°F. Butter a 12 x 6 inch baking pan.

In a bowl, mix the garlic, basil, cream, salt, pepper, eggs, and parsley.

Place the bread in the prepared pan. Add the cheese, then pour the liquid mixture over all.

Place in a pan of water and bake for 35 – 45 minutes or until a toothpick inserted in the center comes out clean.

Yield: 16 side-dish servings

· · · · · · · · · ·
BELOW: *The Vail Cascade Hotel and Club is the community's only AAA Four Diamond ski-in/ ski-out hotel.*

The Lodge and Spa at Cordillera

A t some mountain spas, the snowy peaks are the focus: the slopes beckon, fresh powder taunts, trails challenge. But at The Lodge and Spa at Cordillera the mountains are just part of the picture.

Both skiers and non-skiers have a dream vacation in this secluded getaway located a 20-minute drive from Vail. Winter athletes find plenty of diversion, from downhill skiing at Vail and Beaver Creek to dogsledding, cross-country ski-skating, and snowshoeing.

But for those who want to enjoy the mountains only as a spectacular backdrop, Cordillera packs a world-class spa into its 56-room lodge. With endless views of the Sawatch Mountains, the emphasis at this spa — everywhere from the reception area to the glass-enclosed lap pool — is on comfort and tranquility.

The spa offers a Whole Body Wellness Plan, an all-inclusive week-long vacation that includes hydrotherapy bath, body-wrap, full-body massage, affinoderm body wrap, European facial, five personal training sessions, three aerobics classes, two aqua-exercise classes, and nutrition consultation. Guests can also opt for à la carte treatments — from manicures to texturizing body wraps to aromatherapy.

Restaurant Picasso features a spa menu, with standards such as 262-calorie chicken Cordon Bleu, 191-calorie shrimp linguini, and 250-calorie tandoori chicken. A stay at Cordillera need not be an exercise in calorie-counting, however. Restaurant Picasso also features light French cuisine with dishes carefully prepared by chef Fabrice Beaudoin.

The deluxe style of Cordillera is evident in the accommodations. One of the most lavish features is its Butler Service, available in the four-, five-, and six-bedroom suites. A butler answers the telephone, serves cocktails, presses clothes, schedules activities, and does anything else to ensure that guests enjoy every minute of their vacation of luxury high in the Rocky Mountains.

ABOVE: The resort's world-class spa is one of its most popular features.

AT A GLANCE: *56 rooms with private balcony, mountain view, most with fireplace. 3 restaurants, cooking courses, fitness center, spa, steam room, sauna, whirlpool, beauty salon, indoor / outdoor pool, tennis, volleyball, badminton, croquet, golf, mountain bicycling, hiking, nature walking, horseback riding, cross-country skiing / ski-skating, sleigh rides.* NEARBY: *shops, movie theaters, hot-air ballooning, river rafting, fishing, downhill skiing, snowboarding, skating, snowmobiling, dogsledding.*

Roquefort Pâté

This appetizer, a creation of chef Fabrice Beaudoin, is served at Restaurant Picasso.

2 cups crumbled Roquefort cheese, at room temperature
½ cup butter or margarine, at room temperature
½ cup roasted chopped pecans
½ cup diced dried figs

Combine the cheese and butter. Using a fork, gently mix in the pecans and figs (do not overmix). Place in a medium-sized terrine mold and refrigerate for 8 hours or overnight.

Note: This pâté is excellent served with port sauce. Heat 2 cups of port wine until it reduces to ¼ cup or until syrupy. Pour onto a serving dish. Unmold the terrine and set it in the sauce.

Yield: 8 appetizer servings

Shrimp Cakes

Chef Tab Walla oversees the preparation of these cakes, which are served as an appetizer at the golf club's Timber Hearth Grille.

Sauce:
1 bunch cilantro, chopped
5 garlic cloves, chopped
1 tablespoon grated ginger
1 cup olive oil

Shrimp Cakes:
2 pounds medium-sized shrimp, finely chopped
1 medium red bell pepper, seeded and finely chopped
1 bunch green onions, thinly sliced
2 tablespoons chopped cilantro
2 eggs, lightly beaten

Pinch of salt and pepper
2 cups bread crumbs
Vegetable oil
Butter

Prepare the sauce. Mix all the ingredients.

Prepare the shrimp cakes. Mix the shrimp, bell pepper, onion, cilantro, and beaten eggs. Add the salt and pepper and the bread crumbs. The mixture should be firm and easy to shape into cakes.

In a non-stick pan, using a mixture of half oil and half butter, fry the cakes until browned on both sides.

Serve with the sauce.

Yield: 6 – 7 (appetizer-sized) cakes

· · · · · · · · ·
ABOVE: *The secluded Lodge and Spa at Cordillera is located just a short drive from Vail.*

Heritage Inn

W hether it's a picturesque New England autumn, a powdery white winter, a pristine spring, or a balmy summer, the Heritage Inn is always in season. This resort keeps its guests happy in a classic setting that boasts all the amenities of a large resort.

Southbury,
Connecticut

(800) 932-3466

$

golf

Set in the rolling hills surrounding historic Southbury, nestled amidst some of the finest antiquing in New England, the Heritage Inn overlooks the Pomperaug River. A stay here can be as relaxing or as active as the vacationer fancies.

The Heritage Inn is noted for its excellent resort amenities, such as 27 holes of championship golf. Tennis and both indoor and outdoor swimming are also available. Those who opt for bicycling, jogging, cross-country skiing, or horseback riding appreciate the unspoiled Connecticut countryside. Autumn hayrides through the rolling, wooded hills provide enjoyment for the whole family.

Indoors, the Sports Club, a state-of-the-art facility, keeps guests on the move with racquetball, exercise classes, and Universal circuit training. Their efforts will be rewarded with a therapeutic massage or a soothing whirlpool bath, perhaps topped off with a session in the sauna or the steam room (this inn features separate saunas and steam rooms for men and women).

The Heritage Inn is renowned for its fine restaurant, Timbers on the Green, with high cathedral ceiling, dramatic floor-to-ceiling windows, massive stone hearth, and rustic wood accents. This restaurant features contemporary American fare. Executive chef Don McCradic delights diners with his unique culinary style, which draws from Mexican, Italian, Mediterranean, American Southwestern, and Pacific Northwestern cuisines. For a lighter menu, guests can relax at the pub and grill, which offers 10 beers on tap.

AT A GLANCE: *160 rooms with river view; 3 suites with Jacuzzi, river view. 2 restaurants, fitness center, steam room, sauna, Jacuzzi, beauty salon, shops, indoor/outdoor (heated) pool, day/night tennis, golf, bicycling, rollerblading, fishing, hayrides.* NEARBY: *cooking courses, spa, movie theaters, indoor tennis, hiking, nature walking, horseback riding, hot-air ballooning, windsurfing, boating, river rafting, hunting, downhill/cross-country skiing, snowboarding, skating, snowshoeing, snowmobiling, sleigh rides.*

ABOVE: *This tasteful eastern resort is noted for its championship golf.*

Crab-Filled Trout with Roasted Pepper Coulis

Roasted Pepper Coulis (yields 1½ cups):
4 roasted red bell peppers, peeled and
  seeded (see note)
½ cup olive oil
¼ cup balsamic vinegar
Salt and pepper

Crab-Filled Trout:
½ cup mayonnaise
1 tablespoon Dijon mustard
½ cup bread crumbs
1 tablespoon lemon juice
8 ounces blue crabmeat (preferably
  fresh, picked of all shell fragments)
2 scallions, minced
2 tablespoons minced roasted red bell
  pepper
1 tablespoon finely chopped basil
  leaves, plus some whole leaves for
  garnish
Pinch of paprika
Salt and pepper to taste
4 (10-ounce) boneless trout
All-purpose flour
Olive oil

Prepare the coulis. Purée the roasted pepper with the oil and vinegar until smooth. Strain through a fine strainer. Season to taste.

Prepare the fish. Preheat the oven to 350°F. Combine the mayonnaise, mustard, bread crumbs, and lemon juice. Mix thoroughly. Fold in the crab, scallion, bell pepper, chopped basil, paprika, and salt and pepper.

Season the trout with salt and pepper and fill with the deviled crab mixture. Close tight and tie the head end with butcher's twine. Lightly flour the trout. Heat a sauté pan and coat it in oil. Brown the trout lightly on both sides, then bake it in the oven until cooked through. Remove the twine.

To serve, pour the roasted pepper coulis on each plate. Place the trout in the center of the plate and garnish with the basil leaves.

Note: To roast the pepper, place under a broiler or hold over a gas burner until charred, steam in a sealed plastic bag for 10 minutes (to facilitate peeling), then peel and seed.

Yield: 4 servings

. . . .
ABOVE: *The Heritage Inn is the very definition of classic New England hideaway.*

Amelia Island Plantation

· ·

Amelia Island overlooks the waters of the Atlantic from a perch that has welcomed visitors since 1600 BC. The verdant isle is draped with giant oaks and sprinkled with marshes and lagoons.

· · · · · · · · · ·

Amelia Island, Florida

(800) 874-6878 or (904) 261-6161

$$

beach

The site was first discovered by the Timucuan Indians, who stayed on this barrier island for 2,800 years. Today Amelia Island, located in northeast Florida, is home to both vacationers and wildlife such as sea turtles, raccoons, herons, and egrets. The 1,250-acre Amelia Island Plantation offers visitors a chance to wander its beaches in search of shells, enjoy a wide variety of activities such as golf or tennis, or just relax and do nothing at all. Families are especially welcome here. A supervised youth program helps ensure that every member of the family has fun.

Amelia Island is also home to historic Fernandina Beach, an 1800s fishing village featuring an unusually extensive collection of Victorian buildings. Visitors can spend a day touring the oldest standing plantation in Florida, learning more about the island at the local museum, or perusing the galleries that line the main street.

Whether your days are spent horseback riding, scouting for wildlife, being pampered in the spa, or catching up on your reading beneath a tall oak, innovative dining awaits. The resort's signature restaurant, The Amelia Inn, offers lovely sea views along with its contemporary cuisine. The Verandah, a family-style restaurant, features fresh fish and pastas. Other dining choices are a fast-food spot popular with families, a sports bar, and a restaurant in the golf shop.

· · · · · · · · · ·

ABOVE: *Amelia Island features a beach that seems endless.*

AT A GLANCE: *107 rooms, 128 suites, and 11 deluxe units, all with private balcony, ocean view; 434 villas with private balcony / patio, ocean view. 4 restaurants, fitness center, spa, steam room, sauna, whirlpool, beauty salon, shops, supervised children's programs, indoor / outdoor (heated) pool, day / night tennis, golf, bicycling, rollerblading, hiking, nature walking, horseback riding, beach, watersports, fishing.* NEARBY: *cooking courses, movie theaters, marina, boating, river rafting, skating.*

Broiled Jumbo Shrimp with Mango Chutney

This dish, the signature recipe of Amelia Island Plantation, can be served as an appetizer or entrée.

Mango Chutney (yields 2 cups):
4 ripe mangoes, peeled, pitted, and thinly sliced
½ red bell pepper, very finely diced
¾ cup raisins
½ cup apple cider vinegar
½ cup brown sugar
1 teaspoon grated nutmeg
1 teaspoon ground cloves

Marinade:
1½ cups soy sauce
¼ cup dry white wine
2 teaspoons chopped ginger
2 teaspoons chopped garlic
2 teaspoons chopped mixed herbs (such as parsley, chives, and dill)

Shrimp:
24 fresh jumbo shrimp, peeled and deveined

Prepare the mango chutney. Mix all the ingredients and refrigerate for 8 hours or overnight. (Store any remaining chutney in a tightly sealed jar in the refrigerator.)

Prepare the marinade. Combine all the ingredients and marinate the shrimp for 1 hour. Remove the shrimp and grill to taste.

To serve, place the chutney in the center of each plate. Arrange the shrimp around it.

Yield: 12 appetizer servings or 4 entrée servings

BELOW: *Soothing spa treatments, challenging sports, and innovative cuisine await visitors to Amelia Island.*

The Biltmore Hotel and Golf Resort

T he name Biltmore has long been synonymous with the most glamorous period in Miami history — the days of beauty pageants and aquatic shows, movie stars and gangsters.

Coral Gables, Florida

(800) 727-1926 or (800) 228-3000

$$

golf/spa/tennis

This historic hotel has played host to such famous and infamous people as Bing Crosby, Judy Garland, the Duke and Duchess of Windsor, and Al Capone, who came to enjoy the Florida sunshine in this Mediterranean-style palace.

But The Biltmore, which opened its doors in 1926, later fell on hard times and in 1942 was taken over by the federal government and converted to a military hospital. Following a $55-million renovation the hotel rose to its former glory in 1987.

Today, the world once again comes to The Biltmore's doors for both galas and getaways. Guests find a resort that's more spectacular than ever, boasting gourmet dining, a deluxe spa, challenging golf, and that special Biltmore cachet.

One of the most splendid features of this resort is also its biggest: the Biltmore pool, perhaps the largest swimming pool in the continental United States. Here, Esther Williams and Johnny "Tarzan" Weissmuller performed in aquatic shows. Weissmuller was once a swimming instructor at The Biltmore, and even won a gold medal in the U.S. diving championships in this very pool. Today it features private cabanas for guests to rent, each paved in coral stone and resplendent with tropical blooms.

The fitness center and spa will not disappoint. The full gamut of spa body treatments is available: Swedish, shiatsu, deep tissue, neuromuscular, and aromatherapy massage as well as reflexology and hydrotherapy. Fitness buffs will find state-of-the-art equipment as well as classes in yoga, t'ai chi, aerobics, and aqua aerobics.

Dining provides another chance for visitors to treat themselves. The Courtyard features Caribbean and Southwestern dishes, as well as steak and seafood on the evening menu. The signature restaurant, Il Ristorante, serves fine French-Italian cuisine.

ABOVE: This famous resort boasts gourmet dining, a posh spa, and challenging golf.

AT A GLANCE: *280 rooms with pool/golf course view; 35 suites with private balcony/patio, pool/golf course view; 2 tower suites, 1 with whirlpool, fireplace. 4 restaurants, cooking courses, fitness center, spa, steam room, sauna, beauty salon, shops, outdoor pool, day/night tennis, golf.* NEARBY: *movie theaters, bicycling, rollerblading, beach, scuba diving, snorkeling, windsurfing, boating, marina, fishing.*

Grilled Veal Chops with Madeira-Morel Sauce

Marinade:
2 teaspoons chopped rosemary
2 teaspoons chopped thyme
2 teaspoons salt
2 teaspoons pepper
¼ cup olive oil

Madeira-Morel Sauce:
4 shallots, sliced
Cracked black pepper
Chopped rosemary to taste
8 tablespoons butter
4 cups Madeira
2 cups demi-glace (available in
    specialty food shops)
Salt and pepper to taste
2 cups dried morels, soaked in Madeira
    until soft

Chops:
4 (8 – 10-ounce) veal chops

Garnish:
4 sprigs of rosemary

Prepare the marinade. Mix all the ingredients. Marinate the chops for 4 hours.

Meanwhile, prepare the sauce. Sauté the shallot, pepper, rosemary, and 4 tablespoons of the butter. Add the Madeira and reduce by half. Add the demi-glace and reduce by a quarter. Add the salt and pepper and strain, then stir in the remaining 4 tablespoons of butter. In a separate pan, sauté the morels, seasoned with salt and pepper. Add the Madeira reduction.

Grill the chops to the desired degree and serve with the sauce. Garnish each plate with a sprig of rosemary.

Yield: 4 servings

ABOVE: *The Biltmore dates back to the most glamorous period in Miami history.*

Little Palm Island

I imagine your very own tropical island — a hideaway where you can forget your cares beneath the thatched roof of a private bungalow and spend your days lazing in a hammock or strolling among towering palms.

Little Torch Key, Florida

(800) 3-GET-LOST

$$$$

beach

Since 1988, Little Palm Island has made that dream a reality for vacationers in the Lower Florida Keys. "Little Palm Island was designed with a specific goal in mind," says Ben Woodson, managing partner. "Our prime objective is to offer our guests an intimate, secluded island hideaway where they can completely detach themselves from the pressures of everyday life while enjoying the luxury and superb cuisine of an exclusive resort."

What guests find at Little Palm Island is a getaway where nature and deluxe surroundings go hand in hand to provide a truly one-of-a-kind experience. Every convenience of a prestigious hotel is available, all in a setting of tropical flora and fauna.

After a day of various watersport activities, guests can indulge in relaxing body treatments at The Spa. Massages, facials, manicures, pedicures, and other services are available.

Dining ranks as a top attraction at Little Palm Island. The Great House offers delicacies such as yellow-tailed snapper fillet with fire-roasted bell pepper, pan-fried cornmeal-crusted grouper with sweet-pickle Chardonnay sauce, and superb rack of lamb.

This resort welcomes children 12 years and older.

ABOVE: *Vacationers forget their cares at this tropical hideaway in the Lower Florida Keys.*

AT A GLANCE: *30 suites with Jacuzzi, private balcony, ocean view. Restaurant, cooking courses, fitness center, spa, sauna, whirlpool, shops, outdoor (heated) pool, beach, scuba diving, snorkeling, windsurfing, boating, marina, fishing.* NEARBY: *movie theaters, day/night tennis, golf.*

Tropical Fruit Granité of Mango, Passion Fruit, Guava, and Champagne

The Great House at Little Palm Island garnishes this refreshing dessert with an orchid.

4 passion fruit (see note 1)
2 mangoes
3 guavas (see note 2)
½ cup Champagne
Crushed ice
4 sprigs of mint

Open the passion fruit and spoon the seeds and flesh into a bowl, reserving the shell and some seeds. Peel and purée the mangoes and guavas and mix with the passion fruit. Strain. Mix in the Champagne.

Turn the mixture into a shallow pan and place in the freezer. After 2 hours check to see whether it is frozen. If so, break up the granité with a strong whisk and keep frozen.

Freeze 4 margarita glasses, then fill them with crushed ice.

Spoon the granité into the passion fruit shells. Place the shells in the glasses. Garnish with the seeds and a sprig of mint.

Note 1: Passion fruit is available fresh March through September in Latin markets and many supermarkets.

Note 2: Guavas are available fresh during the latter half of the year in California, Florida, and Hawaii, or canned in specialty food shops.

Yield: 4 servings

BELOW: *Nature and luxury combine to create a truly one-of-a-kind experience at Little Palm Island.*

The Colony Beach and Tennis Resort

*L*ove may be an undesirable score in tennis, but after visiting
The Colony Beach and Tennis Resort it's tough to describe this
destination in any other terms.

*Longboat Key,
Florida*

(800) 4-COLONY

$$ – $$$$

beach / tennis

Perched on secluded
Longboat Key, this gated
island hideaway pampers
every guest — both those
who gravitate to the resort's
award-winning tennis
facilities and those who
prefer to revel in other
features of the tropical
paradise, such as its glorious
hibiscus-lined paths.

This all-suite resort combines luxurious accommodations with tropical lushness. A
white sandy beach tempts guests with the promise of lazy afternoons or of active days
sailing, windsurfing, or snorkeling.

But The Colony's chief draw is its tennis program. Named the number one tennis
resort in the nation by *Tennis* magazine, The Colony makes it easy for every guest,
regardless of ability, to enjoy the courts. Daily lessons and clinics and complimentary
match-making keep every guest happy. Even the youngest of vacationers has a chance to
pick up a racquet — a complimentary half-hour Tiny Tots Tennis class for ages three to six
is scheduled daily.

Those newly awakened muscles can be soothed at the health spa, which features
separate facilities for men and women. There are massage, neuromuscular therapy, shiatsu
to correct imbalances in energy flow, heated body wraps to detoxify, and facial massages
to tone.

The Colony is also renowned for its fine dining. Three waterfront restaurants offer
diverse menus. The Colony Dining Room specializes in American cuisine and seafood
prepared with local ingredients. For more casual occasions, The Colony Bistro serves
both American and ethnic dishes and The Colony Patio Bar prepares sandwiches and
salads to be taken al fresco with a side order of Florida sunshine.

ABOVE: *This all-suite
resort offers first-class
accommodations in a
lush tropical setting.*

AT A GLANCE: *235 suites with whirlpool, private balcony. 3 restaurants, fitness center, spa, steam room,
sauna, whirlpool, beauty salon, shops, supervised children's programs, outdoor (heated) pool, day / night
tennis, bicycling, nature walking, beach, snorkeling, windsurfing, fishing.* NEARBY: *movie theaters, golf,
rollerblading, hiking, horseback riding, scuba diving, boating, marina.*

Peppercorn-Crusted Atlantic Salmon

½ cup sugar

1 tablespoon raspberry vinegar

1 red onion, halved and cut into
  ¼-inch strips

½ yellow bell pepper, seeded and cut
  into ¼-inch strips

½ red bell pepper, seeded and cut
  into ¼-inch strips

¼ cup mango chutney (see page 87)

4 (7-ounce) Atlantic salmon fillets

2 tablespoons crushed black
  peppercorns

2 tablespoons olive oil

Sprigs of dill

Combine the sugar and vinegar in a small saucepan and place over medium heat until golden brown (do not burn). Add the onion, bell pepper, and chutney. Reduce heat and simmer for 15 minutes. Transfer to a bowl and cool to room temperature.

Preheat the oven to 375°F.

Coat the top of the salmon fillets with the peppercorns. Heat the oil in a large sauté pan over medium-high heat and sear the salmon on both sides. Transfer to a baking sheet (peppercorn side up) and bake for 15 minutes (8 – 10 minutes for medium-rare).

Pour equal amounts of the sauce on each plate and place the salmon on top. Garnish with the sprigs of dill and serve immediately.

Yield: 4 servings

. . . .
BELOW: *Guests of The Colony choose from three airy waterfront restaurants.*

Marriott's Bay Point Resort Village

*W*hat do you get when you combine the excellent golf opportunities of Palm Springs, the beach and family fun of Miami, and the atmosphere and charm of the Deep South?

Panama City Beach, Florida

(800) 874-7105 or (904) 234-3307

$

beach / golf

Marriott's Bay Point Resort Village, that's what. Located within a natural wildlife sanctuary in northwest Florida, this family and golf resort offers the attractions of many other destinations served up with Southern charm. One of the resort's unique features is its boat connections for guests to the secluded beaches of Shell Island, a former Spanish settlement, Confederate prison, and gambling casino that now offers a taste of Florida "the way it used to be."

Beach buffs will also enjoy Alligator Point, where jet-skiing, water-skiing, and volleyball keep active guests happy and content. Others might prefer deep-sea fishing, tennis, bicycling, or strolling on the miles of paths that criss-cross this eleven-hundred-acre resort.

But for many vacationers golf is the top draw of Marriott's Bay Point Resort Village. Two championship courses challenge the skills of even the most seasoned players. *Golf Digest* has named Lagoon Legend the second most challenging course in the United States. The more forgiving Club Meadows course has rolling, manicured greens. Two clubhouses, two putting greens, and a driving range will fill the needs of every golfer, no matter what the level.

Dining opportunities are as diverse as the recreational activities here, with eating spots for sun worshippers and golf lovers alike. The star attraction is Stormy's Grille, overlooking St. Andrews Bay and the closing holes of the Lagoon Legend course. It features steaks and grilled seafood.

AT A GLANCE: *273 rooms and 82 suites, all with private balcony / patio, bay / golf course view. 5 restaurants, cooking courses, fitness center, steam room, sauna, whirlpool, beauty salon, shops, supervised children's programs, indoor / outdoor (heated) pool, day / night tennis, basketball, golf, pedal / electric bicycling, hiking, nature walking, beach, scuba diving, snorkeling, boating, marina, fishing, dolphin encounters, beach volleyball, aqua aerobics, video arcade.* NEARBY: *movie theaters.*

ABOVE: *This resort is located in a wildlife sanctuary.*

Grilled Salmon with Wild Rice Croquettes and Red Pepper Coulis

Stormy's Grille serves this dish with steamed asparagus on a bed of mixed greens, garnished with a tomato rose or an edible flower such as a nasturtium or chive flower.

Wild Rice Croquettes (yields 40 croquettes):
1¼ cups wild rice
3½ cups water
6 tablespoons butter
¼ cup all-purpose flour
2½ cups milk
¼ cup chopped shallot
¾ cup minced ham
2 tablespoons chopped parsley
Mace to taste
Salt and pepper to taste
All-purpose flour
Egg wash (2 eggs whipped with 2 tablespoons water)
¼ cup plain bread crumbs

Red Pepper Coulis (yields 3 cups):
3 large red bell peppers, roasted, peeled, and seeded (see note on page 85)
½ cup chicken stock
2 tablespoons soft butter
Salt and pepper to taste

Salmon:
4 (3-ounce) salmon fillets
Olive oil
Salt and cracked pepper to taste

Assembly:
4 sprigs of rosemary

Prepare the croquettes. Cook the rice in the water until open but firm. Make a béchamel sauce using 4 tablespoons of the butter, then adding the flour to make a roux. Add the milk and bring to a boil. Reduce heat and simmer for 15 minutes. Sauté the shallots and ham in the remaining 2 tablespoons of butter. Add the rice, parsley, mace, and salt and pepper. Mix in the béchamel sauce and let cool.

Using a pastry bag fitted with a ¾-inch plain tube, pipe out long strips of the mixture. Freeze (to add texture). When ready to serve, thaw and cut into 2-inch rounds. Roll in the flour. Dip in the egg wash, then the bread crumbs. Deep fry.

Prepare the coulis. Purée the bell peppers in a blender or food processor. Bring the pepper purée and the chicken stock to a simmer and reduce to desired consistency. Strain the mixture through a cheesecloth and blend in the butter. Season.

Prepare the salmon. Rub it with the oil, season, and grill for 4 minutes each side.

To assemble, arrange the salmon on each plate. Spear three croquettes with a sprig of rosemary and place next to the fish. Dot with the red pepper coulis, or serve the coulis on the side. (See front cover photo for suggested presentation.)

Yield: 4 servings

The Cloister

D eciding to visit The Cloister is the easy part. Deciding what to do when you get there . . . now, that's another matter. The Cloister's list of activities is truly dizzying.

Sea Island, Georgia

(800) SEA ISLA

$$$$

beach / golf / spa / tennis

Golf aficionados will love this resort for its 36 holes — along with an additional 18 at the adjacent St. Simons Island Club, which is available to guests of The Cloister. Once part of an antebellum plantation, these courses are approached by the Avenue of the Oaks, a stately walk among towering live oaks that sets the stage for a memorable round of golf. The courses themselves offer seaside vistas, rolling fairways, and blooming plants that explode with color in the spring months.

If tennis is your game, you'll find 18 courts as well as an automated court for practice. Skeet? Three ranges offer guests a chance to try their skills. Those vacationers eager to get out on the water have plenty of options as well.

The Sea Island Spa offers full-service spa facilities and treatments, many echoing the rejuvenating and healthful aspects of the sea. Thalassotherapy, a seaweed wrap, is a popular choice, as are sea-salt scrubs and seaweed gel facials. Other choices include aromatherapy, massage, reflexology, paraffin hand and foot treatments, and hydrotherapy. Exercise classes are offered in every form, from yoga to aerobics.

For many guests, however, the best exercise is that long-time resort favorite, ballroom dancing. And The Cloister claims to be America's foremost resort for ballroom dancing.

Breakfast is served in the main dining room and at the Beach Club. Lunch is taken at the Beach Club or one of the golf clubs, or, during cooler months, in the main dining room. On Friday night a special outdoor plantation supper is served on Rainbow Island. Accommodation includes all meals.

Gourmands might like to mark The Cloister's Food and Wine Classic on their calendars. For close to two decades this mid-January event has been offering guests the opportunity to participate in wine tastings and to sample the best in gourmet dishes. Guest chefs from resorts across the country bring their innovative cooking styles to The Cloister for the annual event.

ABOVE: *Set amid blooming plants, this action-packed resort features golf, tennis, bicycling, horseback riding, and even skeet.*

AT A GLANCE: *262 rooms and 28 suites, some with private balcony / patio, ocean view. 4 restaurants, cooking courses, fitness center, spa, steam room, sauna, beauty salon, shops, supervised children's programs, ballroom dancing, outdoor (heated) pool, tennis, golf, bicycling, nature walking, horseback riding, beach, scuba diving, snorkeling, windsurfing, boating, kayaking, marina, fishing. NEARBY: movie theaters, hunting.*

Pork Loin with Tangerine Sauce

Pork:

**2 pounds pork loin, center cut, well
    trimmed**

Salt and pepper to taste

Tangerine Sauce:

¼ cup sugar

¼ cup cider vinegar

1 cup tangerine or orange juice

1 ounce plus a few drops of dry sherry

2 tablespoons orange marmalade

Final preparation:

**6 tangerines, mandarin oranges, or
    loquats (see note)**

1 carrot, coarsely chopped

1 onion, coarsely chopped

2 celery stalks, coarsely chopped

Cornstarch

Preheat the oven to 325°F.

Prepare the pork. Season with salt and pepper. Place in a thoroughly warmed roasting pan and roast on the stovetop for about 10 minutes, then place in the oven, fat side up so that it will self-baste. Roast for 60 minutes or until it reaches an internal temperature of 160°F.

Meanwhile, prepare the tangerine sauce. In a heavy-bottomed saucepan, cook the sugar to a golden color. Add the vinegar, tangerine juice, and sherry. Stand back, as the sugar will boil furiously and emit steam. Stir in the marmalade. Keep the sauce simmering until the pork is done.

Finish preparing the pork. Add the tangerines to the roasting pork long enough to heat them through. Place the roast on a serving platter and surround it with the tangerines. Put the roasting pan on the stovetop over high heat. Add the carrot, onion, and celery. Sauté for 3 – 5 minutes to get the drippings; carefully pour off the fat. Add the tangerine sauce. Adjust the seasoning. A small amount of cornstarch mixed with sherry may be needed to thicken the sauce. Strain and discard the vegetables.

Pour some of the sauce over the roast and the fruit; serve the remainder in a saucière.

Note: The loquat, also known as the May apple, Japanese medlar, or Japanese plum, is slightly pear-shaped and resembles an apricot in size and color. This sweetly tart fruit is available fresh only in regions where it is grown (in North America, only California and Florida). It is available dried or canned in Asian markets.

Yield: 6 servings

Below: *The Cloister stretches along Sea Island.*

The Orchid at Mauna Lani

*T*he beauty of the Kohala Coast on the Island of Hawaii may initially attract vacationers to this resort, but the fine dining could very well keep them coming back.

Chef David Reardon, who heads up three restaurants at this tropical getaway, is co-founder of the ITT Sheraton's Cuisine of the Americas. This program focuses on the diversity of seasonings and cooking styles from across the Western Hemisphere, offering dishes low in fat and calories.

At The Grill, Reardon serves dishes that showcase the unique flavorings of Hawaii. The menu features sumptuous offerings like guava-grilled pork tenderloin, Kohala mixed grill with mahimahi, and pesto-grilled ahi tuna. The Orchid Court focuses on the many cuisines of the Pacific Rim, while Brown's Beach House serves Hawaiian regional dishes with a California twist.

But dining is just one of many attractions at The Orchid at Mauna Lani. A deluxe spa features relaxing therapies as well as a variety of exercise classes. The Spa Without Walls program makes use of the sprawling resort grounds to offer treatments and classes in the great outdoors. Guests can have a massage on the pounding shoreline, a yoga session on the sandy beach, a power walk through ancient volcano flows, or a t'ai chi class beneath towering palms.

The Orchid at Mauna Lani offers 36 holes of golf in an exotic setting. The north course includes a rolling form of lava called pāhoehoe, while the south course features two signature ocean holes.

ABOVE: *Watersports, tennis, and championship golf keep guests in shape . . . and the spa awaits.*

AT A GLANCE: *539 rooms and 54 suites, all with private balcony, garden/mountain/ocean view. 3 restaurants, fitness center, spa, steam room, sauna, whirlpool, beauty salon, shops, supervised children's programs, outdoor (heated) pool, day/night tennis, golf, bicycling, rollerblading, hiking, nature walking, beach, scuba diving, snorkeling.*

Banana-Chocolate Bread Pudding with Caramel Sauce and Coffee Ice Cream

The Orchid at Mauna Lani uses its own Kona coffee ice cream in this dessert dish.

Banana Bread (yields 1 loaf):
2 cups cake flour
1 tablespoon baking powder
½ teaspoon salt
¼ teaspoon grated nutmeg
½ cup butter
¼ cup granulated sugar
¼ cup brown sugar
1 egg, beaten
1 pound ripe bananas, mashed
1 teaspoon vanilla

Chocolate Custard:
⅔ cup whipping cream
½ pound bittersweet chocolate
¼ cup diced butter
2⅓ cups milk
3 eggs
3 egg yolks
¾ cup brown sugar

Caramel Sauce:
½ cup sugar
¼ cup whipping cream

Glazed Banana:
3 bananas, thinly sliced
¼ cup brown sugar

Coffee ice cream
Fresh berries
Mint leaves

Prepare the bread. Preheat the oven to 350°F. Grease an 8 x 4 x 4-inch loaf pan.

Mix the flour, baking powder, salt, and nutmeg. Cream the butter and sugar. Gradually beat in the egg. Add the banana, then fold in the dry ingredients and blend until smooth. Mix in the vanilla. Turn the mixture into the prepared pan and bake for 50 minutes or until a knife inserted in the center comes out clean.

Prepare the chocolate custard. Bring the cream to a boil, then pour it over the chocolate and the butter. Mix until smooth. Place in a saucepan. Add the milk and cook, stirring, over medium heat until thoroughly combined. Remove from heat. In a stainless steel bowl, whisk the eggs, egg yolks, and sugar. Add the chocolate mixture and whisk. Strain through a fine sieve.

Cut the banana bread into 1-inch cubes. Place in a large bowl and cover with the chocolate custard. Cover with plastic wrap and let stand for 30 minutes or until the bread has soaked up the custard. Preheat the oven to 375°F. Grease 12 (4-ounce) tin cups or ramekins and place in a deep baking pan half filled with water. Fill each cup three quarters full and bake for 15 minutes or until set. Let cool for 5 minutes, then remove from the cups.

Prepare the caramel sauce. In a heavy saucepan, cover the sugar with water and cook over low heat until dissolved. Increase the heat and boil until the sugar caramelizes and is deep brown (do not let it burn). Gradually pour in the cream. Simmer, stirring occasionally, until smooth and thick. Cool.

Prepare the glazed banana. Overlap the banana slices in a circle. Sprinkle with the sugar and broil until brown (or use a torch).

To serve, place the warm bread pudding in the center of each plate. Top with the glazed banana, then a scoop of the ice cream. Drizzle with the caramel sauce and garnish with a few berries and a mint leaf.

Yield: 12 servings

Big Cedar Lodge

An Ozark day begins just as it has for centuries: an early-morning haze blankets the valleys, birds come out to greet the dawn, the light slowly penetrates the thick cover of the forest.

Ridgedale, Missouri

(417) 335-2777

$

fishing / golf

Travelers who have visited the Rockies or the Smokies should not expect to see many similarities between these landscapes and the Ozarks — at least as far as the mountains are concerned. There's a saying in the Ozarks that perfectly sums up this terrain: "Our hills ain't high, our hollers is just deep."

Today, several of those hollers are filled with lakes that tempt fishermen to try their luck. Table Rock Lake is rated among the top five bass lakes in the United States. And in a tranquil cove of the lake you'll find Big Cedar Lodge, one of the finest accommodations in the Ozarks.

Big Cedar actually encompasses Valley View Lodge, Knotty Pine Cottages, Spring View, which faces Table Rock Lake, and the main facility of Falls Lodge. Private log cabins for two to six adults are also available. The accommodations feature stone fireplace and antique furnishings, as well as an unmistakable lodge atmosphere.

Fishing ranks as a top activity here, but it's by no means the only form of fun. A new Jack Nicklaus signature par 3 golf course, Top of the Rock, offers views of Table Rock Lake. Equestrian activities keep riders and non-riders occupied, with everything from carriage rides to horseback trails. And for those ready to do some local exploring, nearby Branson has three outlet malls, a theme park, and country music shows that light up the town every night.

After a day of activity, guests like to dine at the Devil's Pool Restaurant overlooking a peaceful cove of Table Rock Lake.

ABOVE: Hidden in a quiet cove of Table Rock Lake, this full-service resort caters to every interest.

AT A GLANCE: *145 rooms, 10 suites, and 90 cabins, all with Jacuzzi, fireplace, private balcony / patio, scenic view. 3 restaurants, cooking courses, fitness center, steam room, sauna, whirlpool, shops, supervised children's programs, outdoor (heated) pool, day / night tennis, golf, hiking, nature walking, horseback riding, watersports, boating, marina, fishing.* NEARBY: *beauty salon, movie theaters, indoor pool, indoor tennis, bicycling, beach, scuba diving, snorkeling.*

Pineapple Upside-Down French Toast Casserole

½ cup butter

¼ cup maple syrup, plus extra for
   serving

½ cup plus 1 tablespoon brown sugar

1 pineapple cut into chunks

½ cup raisins

8 eggs

1½ cups milk

2 teaspoons vanilla

1 loaf Italian or French bread, sliced
   diagonally

Preheat the oven to 350°F. Grease an 11 x 14-inch baking pan.

Melt the butter, the ¼ cup of maple syrup, and the ½ cup of sugar together over low heat. Pour into the prepared pan and sprinkle evenly with the pineapple and raisins.

Mix the eggs, milk, vanilla, and the remaining 1 tablespoon of sugar until smooth. Thoroughly soak the bread in the batter, then arrange the slices over the pineapple and raisins in the pan. Bake for 35 minutes.

Cut into squares and invert on each plate. Serve immediately, with maple syrup.

Yield: 10 servings

. . . .
BELOW: *Big Cedar Lodge encompasses several rustic lodges and cabins.*

The Bishop's Lodge

Adjacent to the Santa Fe National Forest and just three miles from the city of Santa Fe, this historic inn represents the best of both country and city getaways.

*Santa Fe,
New Mexico*

(800) 732-2240

$$

mountain

Guests can start their mornings with a crisp walk beneath towering cottonwood and oak trees, enjoy an afternoon of horseback riding, then relax with a gourmet meal followed by a visit to the Santa Fe Opera.

This site dates back to the days before Santa Fe became a Southwestern hot spot for both its cuisine and its culture. In the late 1800s, Bishop Jean Baptiste Lamy sought a place where he could relax and meditate away from the rigors of life in Santa Fe. He traveled to this site and built his retreat lodge in a style that combined Hispanic, New Mexican, and European elements. After Lamy's death, the property changed ownership several times, eventually falling into the hands of the Pulitzer family of publishing fame. They built two residences, the south and north lodges, when the land had just become part of the newly created 47th state. Eventually Bishop's Lodge was transformed into a resort, although today it is still known for the assets Lamy cherished so long ago: peace and tranquility.

This ranch resort is located on a vast thousand acres of land that give travelers plenty of room to spread out while they contemplate nature in a pristine Southwestern environment. Horseback riding, offered from April through November, is a popular way to survey the ranch, as is hiking on its many trails. Guests have a chance to spot local wildlife: rabbits, horned toads, coyotes, mule deer, raccoons, and Great Horned Owls.

After a day of adventure, vacationers can try New American cuisine at the Bishop's Lodge Restaurant. The menu tends to vary but always includes such dishes as crab cakes with corn and avocado relish, ranch-raised elk noisette with grilled polenta and red cabbage, and almond tuille baskets (see recipe opposite) filled with fresh berries.

ABOVE: The Bishop's Lodge has been a place of calm and serenity for more than a century.

AT A GLANCE: *68 rooms and 20 suites, some with fireplace, private patio. Restaurant, fitness center, sauna, whirlpool, supervised children's programs (in summer), outdoor (heated) pool (April — October), tennis (April — October), hiking, nature walking, horseback riding, children's fishing (April — October), skeet shooting.* NEARBY: *cooking courses, beauty salon, shops, movie theaters, golf, bicycling, river rafting, fishing, downhill/cross-country skiing, snowboarding, snowshoeing.*

Almond Tuille Basket

The Bishop's Lodge fills each basket with fresh berries and serves it on a rippled pool of crème anglaise (homemade ice cream or sorbet are good substitutes).

½ cup softened butter
1 cup cake flour
¼ cup corn syrup
1 tablespoon sugar
1 cup sliced almonds

Preheat the oven to 350°F. Lightly grease several baking sheets.

Using an electric mixer, blend the butter and flour until smooth. Add the corn syrup and sugar and continue mixing until creamy. Stir in the almonds.

Using a tablespoon, drop the dough by the 1 – 1½-ounce dollop onto the prepared baking sheet, spaced 6 inches apart. Bake until lightly browned all over, then cool for 2 – 3 minutes. Slide a cake spatula under each cookie and drape it over an inverted soup or cereal bowl (one per cookie), pressing the sides down to form a basket. Cool for 5 minutes before removing and storing in an airtight container. If cookies harden and are not pliable, return them to the oven for 1 – 2 minutes or until soft enough to drape over the bowls.

Yield: 12 – 15 baskets

Dijon-Crusted Salmon on Arugula with Dill Vinaigrette

4 (5-ounce) salmon fillets
Salt, pepper, and/or sugar to taste
2 tablespoons powdered mustard
¾ cup olive oil
2 tablespoons Dijon mustard

¼ cup cider vinegar
4 tablespoons snipped dill
Arugula leaves

Season the fillets. Mix the powdered mustard with ¼ cup of the oil, then add the Dijon mustard. Spread evenly over one side of the fillets. Let stand for 30 minutes.

Heat another ¼ cup of the oil in a cast-iron sauté pan and cook the fillets for 2 – 3 minutes per side (mustard side first).

To make the vinaigrette, mix the vinegar, remaining ¼ cup of oil, and dill.

Arrange the arugula leaves on each plate and place the salmon fillets over the leaves. Drizzle the vinaigrette over all.

Yield: 4 servings

. . . .
ABOVE: *The delicate almond tuille basket makes a sweet ending to any meal.*

Mirror Lake Inn

When *Mirror Lake Inn suffered a catastrophic fire in January 1988, there was only one solution for husband-and-wife owners Ed and Lisa Weibrecht: rebuild the then 64-year-old structure.*

Lake Placid,
New York

(518) 523-2544

$ – $$$

mountain

The classic inn quickly rose like a phoenix from the ashes, and by Independence Day reopened with the panache befitting this AAA Four Diamond property. Today the resort offers a sporty getaway any time of year.

One reminder of the fire is the Averil Conwell Dining Room. The walls of this restaurant are decorated with the works of Averil Courtney Conwell, a nationally recognized artist who resided in Lake Placid until her death in 1990. The murals of typical Lake Placid scenes were cut from the walls of the dining room as the fire raged. When the inn was reconstructed, Mrs. Conwell, then 94, restored the priceless paintings.

These paintings are not the only works of art in this dining room — every evening, creations such as hickory-smoked shrimp and escargots Napoléon introduce pan-seared salmon fillet, roasted rack of lamb, sautéed trout amaretto, and grilled breast of duck.

Guests have plenty of opportunity to work off the effects of that fine dining. The village of Lake Placid, two-time (1932 and 1980) Winter Olympics host, is home to every imaginable winter sport. Downhill and cross-country skiing or speed and figure skating delight many, and thrill seekers enjoy the one-man luge runs and the year-round chance to have a ride on a bobsled as it speeds down the Olympic track.

The summer months bring a new alpine beauty to Mirror Lake, along with opportunities for hiking, mountain biking, and other fair-weather pursuits along the shores of the lake.

Guests seeking a little romance might check into the split-level suite with king-sized bed and whirlpool for two perched in a loft reached by a spiral staircase; the oak stairs, like all the woodwork, were made by Mirror Lake Inn's own craftspersons. The Adirondack mini-suite on the shores of the lake is filled with custom-made birch-bark furnishings.

*A*BOVE: *A superb getaway any time of year, this resort is resplendent in winter.*

AT A GLANCE: *110 rooms with private balcony, mountain/lake view; 18 suites with whirlpool, mountain/lake view, most with private balcony, some with fireplace. 2 restaurants, fitness center, spa, sauna, whirlpool, beauty salon, indoor/outdoor (heated) pool, tennis, beach, boating, fishing, skating.* N*EARBY: shops, movie theaters, supervised children's programs, golf, bicycling, rollerblading, hiking, nature walking, horseback riding, watersports, marina, hunting, downhill/cross-country skiing, snowboarding, snowshoeing, snowmobiling, dogsledding, sleigh rides.*

Rack of Lamb with Minted Zinfandel Sauce

Rack of Lamb:

1 tablespoon chopped garlic

1 tablespoon chopped rosemary

1 tablespoon olive oil

2 (1-pound) racks of lamb, trimmed
   of fat

Minted Zinfandel Sauce:

2 tablespoons finely chopped shallot

Olive oil

¼ cup mint jelly

2 cups Zinfandel

1 quart demi-glace (available in
   specialty food shops)

2 tablespoons chopped mint

Salt and pepper to taste

Prepare the lamb. Preheat the oven to 375°F. Combine the garlic, rosemary, and oil. Use this to coat the lamb. Roast for about 15 minutes, at 130°F for medium rare, 140°F for medium, or 160°F for well done.

Meanwhile, prepare the sauce. Lightly sauté the shallot in the oil. Add the mint jelly and the wine and reduce the volume by half. Add the demi-glace and cook for 15 minutes. Strain. Garnish with the chopped mint and season with salt and pepper.

Slice the lamb and serve with the sauce.

Yield: 4 servings

LEFT: *Rack of lamb with minted Zinfandel sauce is a perennial favorite in the Averil Conwell Dining Room at lovely Mirror Lake Inn.*

Sunriver Resort

The seasons may change, turning the landscape from green to gold to powdery white, but at Sunriver Resort the activity level never drops. This mountain retreat keeps its guests on the move.

Sunriver, Oregon

*(800) 547-3922 or
(541) 593-1000*

$

golf / mountain

Summer? Time for some horseback riding or white-water rafting. Spring or fall? How about tennis or biking? Winter? Grab some skis and head for the slopes.

But the shining star at Sunriver, located 15 miles south of Bend, is its golf. Often noted as the best golf destination in the Northwest, Sunriver has garnered just about every accolade awarded to golf resorts. Much of the attention is lavished on Woodlands Golf Course, designed by Robert Trent Jones, Jr., with lakes and rock outcroppings to challenge any player. The newest course is Crosswater, designed by Robert Cupp: spectacular mountain views sliced by the Deschutes and Little Deschutes rivers. Sunriver's third course is the Meadows Course, home of the *Golf Digest* schools. These schools operate June through September with programs that run from half a day to three days.

The Meadows Restaurant, which features Northwestern specialties, overlooks the majestic Central Oregon Cascades. Other dining options are McDivot's Café and the Par Patio. The Grille at Crosswater serves superb meals in a rustic setting, with a view of the beautiful Crosswater links as a bonus.

ABOVE: *Whatever the season, Sunriver Resort offers a beautiful western getaway.*

AT A GLANCE: *134 rooms and 77 suites, all with fireplace, private balcony, mountain / forest / golf course view; 250 houses / condos with Jacuzzi, whirlpool, hot tub, fireplace, private balcony, mountain / forest / golf course view. 6 restaurants, cooking courses, fitness center, sauna, whirlpool, beauty salon, shops, supervised children's programs, outdoor (heated) pool, indoor / outdoor tennis, golf, bicycling, hiking, nature walking, horseback riding, watersports, boating, marina, river rafting, fishing, cross-country skiing, skating, snowshoeing, sleigh rides, airport.* NEARBY: *movie theaters, indoor pool, hot-air ballooning, scuba diving, windsurfing, hunting, downhill skiing, snowboarding, snowmobiling, dogsledding.*

Spiced Onion and Ale Soup

Sunriver Resort uses Deschutes Golden Ale and local Tillamook Cheddar cheese in this recipe.

2 tablespoons butter
4 large Walla Walla onions, thinly sliced
   (see note)
¼ cup Dijon mustard
1½ cups golden ale
8 cups chicken stock
2 tablespoons cornstarch dissolved in
   ½ cup cold water
1 cup diced apple-cured bacon,
   cooked until crisp
3 tablespoons minced garlic
¼ teaspoon ground allspice
¼ cup chopped fresh thyme, or
   1 teaspoon dried
Salt and pepper to taste
2 cups grated extra sharp Cheddar
   cheese
½ cup sliced green onion

In a large, heavy saucepan over medium heat, melt the butter and cook the onion on low heat for 12 minutes or until evenly caramelized.

Add the mustard, ale, and stock and simmer for 15 – 20 minutes. Add the cornstarch dissolved in water and boil gently for 3 – 4 minutes. Reduce to a simmer and add the bacon, garlic, allspice, thyme, and salt and pepper.

Garnish with the cheese and green onion.

Note: Named after the Washington city, Walla Walla onions are milder than most. They are in season from June to September but are usually available outside their growing area only by mail order. If necessary, substitute with Maui sweet onions.

Yield: 14 servings

. . . .

BELOW: *Sunriver Resort receives much attention for its unique golfing opportunities.*

Lake Austin Spa Resort

A meal at Lake Austin Spa is reason enough to schedule a stay at this resort, which combines spa luxury with the rustic atmosphere of a lake retreat.

Austin, Texas

(800) 847-5637 or (800) 338-6651

$$ – $$$

spa

Lake Austin Spa Resort proves one thing: just because something's good for you doesn't mean you won't like it. Sure, your mom once chanted, "Eat it, it's good for you," over a plate of tasteless vegetables, but then your mom wasn't Terry Conlan. The head chef of this lakeside resort cooks up a lean, mean menu, one that uses healthy ingredients to draw out the flavors of the Southwest. The author of *Lean Star Cuisine,* Conlan includes among his creations enchiladas verdes, shrimp quesadillas with mango salsa, crab cakes with chipotle mayonnaise, pumpkin flan, and chocolate Kahlúa mousse. It's all served in a dining room that overlooks the waters of Lake Austin.

But plenty of other attractions await. Perched on a tranquil shore of Lake Austin amidst rolling hills, the resort is the very definition of casual elegance. There's an abundance of activity here: dancing, aerobics on a suspended wooden floor, tennis, mountain biking, and even sculling on the calm waters of the lake. Activity goes hand-in-hand with relaxation, and at the Lake Austin Spa that means stress-reduction sessions. For the ultimate in pampering, guests can splurge with aromatherapy, massage, underwater massage, invigorating sea-salt scrub, aloe vera body masque, paraffin body wrap, Moortherapy using 30,000-year-old mud, manicure, facial, and aromatherapy scalp conditioning.

The grounds, which offer a view of a rugged cliff and the sea-green waters of Lake Austin, are as wild as the surrounding Hill Country, with a variety of wildlife and wildflowers.

ABOVE: Guests can while away an afternoon amidst rolling hills.

AT A GLANCE: *40 rooms with scenic view. Restaurant, cooking courses, fitness center, spa, steam room, sauna, whirlpool, shops, indoor/outdoor (heated) pool, day/night tennis, bicycling, hiking, nature walking, beach, watersports, sculling, kayaking, canoeing, marina, fishing.* NEARBY: *beauty salon, movie theaters, indoor tennis, golf, rollerblading, horseback riding, hot-air ballooning, scuba diving, snorkeling, windsurfing, river rafting, hunting.*

Eggplant Enchiladas

Sauce (yields 2 cups):

2 tomatoes

1 small onion, thickly sliced

1 serrano chili, halved and seeded

1 large red bell pepper, roasted, peeled,
　　and seeded (see note on page 85)

3 garlic cloves

2 tablespoons chopped cilantro

Juice of ½ lime

1 teaspoon ground cumin

Enchiladas:

1 cup chopped onion

2 garlic cloves, minced

¼ cup defatted chicken broth

6 cups peeled and cubed eggplant
　　(2 small)

1 cup chopped green bell pepper

1 cup sliced mushrooms

1 teaspoon Worcestershire sauce

2 tablespoons chopped toasted
　　almonds

1 tablespoon minced parsley

1 teaspoon black pepper

1 cup grated low-fat Monterey Jack
　　cheese

Assembly:

12 whole wheat tortillas

Vegetable or chicken stock for
　　softening tortillas

Prepare the sauce. Char the tomatoes, onion, and chili under the broiler or over the flame of a gas burner. Combine all the ingredients in a food processor or blender and process until smooth.

Prepare the enchiladas. In a large sauté pan, sauté the onion and garlic in the broth for 5 minutes. Stir in the eggplant, bell pepper, mushrooms, and Worcestershire sauce. Cook for 10 – 12 minutes or until the eggplant is soft. Remove from heat and add the almonds, parsley, black pepper, and ¾ cup of the cheese.

To assemble, preheat the oven to 350°F. Grease a glass baking dish. Simmer a small amount of stock in a small sauté pan. Dip the tortillas individually, on each side, to soften. Place a portion of the eggplant mixture in each tortilla and roll tightly. Place seam side down in the prepared baking dish. Top with the remaining cheese and bake for 20 minutes. Serve with the sauce.

　　Yield: 12 servings

BELOW: *Lake Austin Spa Resort is simplicity in the best sense of the word.*

Lakeway Inn

Austin, Texas

(800) LAKEWAY

$

golf/tennis

*T*he richest vacation region in Texas was formed in less time than it takes to describe it. The Hill Country, a scenic area west of Austin, was shaped 30 million years ago by a violent earthquake.

It was over in just three and a half minutes, but the convulsion buckled the earth and kicked up strata of limestone and granite into rugged hills and steep cliffs.

Today, several winding lakes nestle in the valleys of those verdant hills. Among these is the 65-mile-long Lake Travis, which snakes through the Hill Country and presses up against the boundaries of Austin and one of the state's top resorts, the Lakeway Inn.

The Lakeway Inn has long attracted golfers to its two 18-hole championship courses: Yaupon and Live Oak. Yaupon challenges players with white sand bunkers that contrast sharply with the groomed fairways. Live Oak utilizes creeks and canyons, bringing the unique Hill Country landscape to the golf course. Golfers eager to improve their game can register at the Jack Nicklaus-designed Academy of Golf, which comprises two schools and three full-length holes.

Off the links, there's no shortage of diversions. Lakeway's full-service marina, for instance, is a hub of activity. Some guests try their luck fishing or take a sailboat and explore some of Lake Travis's scenic coves, which in the spring months are lined with fields of fragrant bluebonnets.

Lakeway is also noted as a tennis center. Home of the World of Tennis complex, it has been rated as one of the top 25 tennis destinations in the world. Professional instruction is available here, and guests shouldn't be surprised to see some tournament action at the Stadium Court, which seats twelve hundred.

After a day of fun, vacationers usually settle back for a delectable meal in the Travis Dining Room overlooking the lake. Among the favorites on its Southwestern menu are tortilla soup (see recipe opposite), lobster enchiladas, Hill Country cobb salad, and even grilled ostrich.

ABOVE: *Golf, tennis, and watersports keep visitors on the move.*

AT A GLANCE: *109 rooms with private balcony/patio, lake/marina view; 28 suites with fireplace, private balcony/patio, lake/marina view. 2 restaurants, fitness center, spa, sauna, whirlpool, outdoor pool, watersports, marina, fishing. NEARBY: steam room, beauty salon, shops, indoor/outdoor/night tennis, golf, bicycling, hiking, nature walking, horseback riding, scuba diving, snorkeling, windsurfing, boating, hunting.*

Tortilla Soup

This Texas favorite from the Lakeway Inn's Travis Dining Room is the creation of executive chef Shawn Witt.

1 medium green bell pepper, seeded
   and chopped
1 yellow onion, chopped
¼ cup chopped cilantro
1¾ pounds diced tomato (3 cups)
1 teaspoon granulated garlic
½ teaspoon white pepper
2 tablespoons ground cumin
3 quarts water
2 chicken bouillon cubes
10 corn tortillas, cut into small strips
   and fried
1 avocado, pitted, peeled, and sliced
2 cups grated Monterey Jack cheese

In a large blender or food processor, purée the bell pepper, onion, and cilantro. Sauté the puréed mixture over medium heat for 5 minutes. Purée the tomato and add it to the bell pepper mixture. Add the garlic, white pepper, and cumin and continue to sauté for 5 minutes. Add the water and bouillon cubes and bring the mixture to a boil. Add the fried tortilla strips. Adjust the seasoning to taste. Garnish with the avocado and cheese.

   Yield: 20 servings

ABOVE: *Springtime vacationers are greeted with fields of fragrant bluebonnets.*

Four Seasons Resort and Club at Las Colinas

E vian spritzers and chilled towels to cool tanning skin. Mornings golfing on a championship course, afternoons luxuriating in a lavish spa and being pampered in a salon, then riding in a limo to Neiman-Marcus, to be greeted by a personal shopping assistant.

Irving, Texas

(800) 332-3442 or (972) 717-0700

$$ – $$$

golf/spa

Dallas-Fort Worth relishes its image — as a result of the long-running television series *Dallas* — as a place of fabulous wealth and opulence. But even oil barons would have a hard time topping the decadence enjoyed, if only briefly, by guests of the Four Seasons Resort and Club at Las Colinas.

Las Colinas, a planned community in the city of Irving just west of Dallas, boasts some of the largest businesses in the world. The Four Seasons was opened in 1986 to accommodate the executives who shuttle in and out of Las Colinas. CEOs can wind down with 18 holes of golf, a game of tennis or squash, and perhaps a Swedish massage followed by a superb meal.

Now others seeking a weekend of indulgence are flocking to the resort. Here, a day might start with breakfast served on a balcony overlooking the vast resort and end with a soak in the bubbling hot tub, steam rising from a waterfall as it splashes over natural stone. Many of the hours in between might be spent golfing. The course winds its way behind the resort, offering views of the hotel, the highrises of Irving, and the rolling prairie. Couples often opt for a round of twilight golf, toting chilled Champagne and caviar in their cart to put a romantic twist on the sport.

The fitness center features racquetball, squash, tennis, half-court basketball, heated swimming pools, indoor and outdoor jogging tracks, and an endless range of exercise classes. The deluxe spa has separate men's and women's sections. You can cocoon yourself in an oversized robe, sip iced spring water, then head for the steam room, sauna, or whirlpool.

Nutritional counseling is available, but the casual dieter can select a healthy meal by looking for the Alternative Cuisine section found on all the Four Seasons menus. Low-fat meals are served in even the resort's toniest restaurant, Café on the Green.

ABOVE: *At the Four Seasons Resort and Club at Las Colinas, guests can relax after a busy day of golf, tennis, racquetball, fitness classes, or spa treatments.*

AT A GLANCE: *344 rooms, some with private balcony/patio, most with golf course/pool view; 18 suites, some with fireplace, private balcony/patio, most with golf course/pool view. 3 restaurants, fitness center, spa, steam room, sauna, whirlpool, beauty salon, shops, supervised children's programs, indoor/outdoor (heated) pool, indoor/outdoor/night tennis, racquetball, golf, indoor/outdoor jogging.* NEARBY: *movie theaters, horseback riding, hot-air ballooning, watersports, windsurfing, boating, marina.*

New York Steak with Tobacco Onions, Anasazi Bean Chili, and Blackstrap Barbecue Sauce

Chef Bernhard Muller oversees the preparation of this dish at Café on the Green.

Anasazi Bean Chili (yields 4 cups):
1 medium onion, chopped
1 red bell pepper, seeded and diced
1 yellow bell pepper, seeded and diced
1 poblano, seeded and diced (see
   note 2 on page 77)
2 ancho chilies, seeded and diced (see
   note 1 on pagc 49)
Vegetable oil
4 garlic cloves, minced
¼ cup mole paste (available in
   Mexican markets or specialty food
   shops)
1 cup anasazi beans, soaked in water
   for 8 hours or overnight
4 tomatoes, peeled and diced
1 teaspoon dried oregano
1 tablespoon ground cumin
1 teaspoon dried thyme
1½ cups beer
Chicken stock, as needed
Salt and pepper to taste

*Blackstrap Barbecue Sauce (yields
   ½ cup):*
1 onion, minced
Vegetable oil
4 garlic cloves, minced
¼ cup red wine vinegar
¼ cup rice vinegar
¼ cup cider vinegar
½ teaspoon ground cloves
½ teaspoon ground allspice
1 teaspoon ground cumin
½ cup blackstrap molasses
¼ cup brown sugar

¼ cup mole paste
1½ cups ketchup
1 teaspoon Worcestershire sauce
Salt and pepper to taste

Tobacco Onions:
1 tablespoon onion powder
1 tablespoon garlic powder
1 teaspoon ground cayenne
1 teaspoon white pepper
½ teaspoon salt
½ teaspoon paprika
2 onions, sliced

Steak:
6 (8-ounce) New York strip steaks
Salt and pepper to taste

Prepare the chili. Brown the onion, bell pepper, poblano, and ancho chili in the oil. Add the garlic and the mole paste and sauté briefly. Add the beans, tomato, oregano, cumin, thyme, and beer. Simmer for 60 – 90 minutes or until the beans are soft, adding stock when needed to maintain moisture. Season.

Prepare the sauce. Sauté the onion in the oil until translucent. Add the garlic and sauté. Add the three vinegars and reduce by half. Add the cloves, allspice, cumin, molasses, sugar, mole paste, ketchup, and Worcestershire sauce and simmer for 20 minutes. Season.

Prepare the onions. Mix the seasonings. Toss with the onion and deep fry until crisp.

Prepare the steak. Season, then grill over medium-hot coals to the desired temperature. Place on a rack to let the internal juices distribute evenly throughout. Keep warm.

To serve, heat the chili and place in the center of each plate. Top with the steak, then the onions. Drizzle the sauce around the plate.

Yield: 6 servings

Hyatt Regency Hill Country Resort

*Y*ou start your day surveying acres of rolling hills from a rocking chair on the wide porch. Inside, some guests sit around an open hearth, while others sleep late in their pine beds.

San Antonio, Texas

(800) 233-1234

$$

golf

No, this isn't a lonely Texas ranch. It's the Hyatt Regency Hill Country Resort, a two-hundred-acre complex that's pure Texas. This resort is located on a former ranch that was family run for more than a century. Dotted with majestic live oaks and sprinkled with limestone and stands of prickly pear cactus, the ranch rolls across the Hill Country, Texas's richest vacation region. The Hill Country was shaped 30 million years ago by an earthquake that lasted just three and a half minutes. The convulsion buckled the land north and west of San Antonio, kicking up strata of limestone and granite into rugged hills and steep cliffs.

The jagged scar of the event, the Balcones Escarpment, zigzags through the state, marking the frontier between flat farmland to the east and rugged ranches to the west. Fields of cotton and corn become hills of limestone scrabble, textured by juniper and live oak and dotted with wildflowers. The resort incorporated these Hill Country features into the design of the low-rise Hyatt.

The expansive lobby resembles that of a grand ranch house, complete with a wall-sized stone fireplace, cowhide chairs, and overstuffed sofas. The ranch motif carries over to the guest rooms, with wall stenciling, ironwork accessories, and tall, carved head-boards. The colors mimic those of the surrounding landscape — the blue of bluebonnets and the red of Indian paintbrush.

The Hill Country Golf Club, an 18-hole championship course, is one of this resort's most popular attractions. The clubhouse is home to Antlers Lodge, which features Southwestern cuisine and an atmosphere casual enough to let diners relax after a day of sightseeing in San Antonio but appealing enough to highlight a night out. Lighter fare is served at the Cactus Oak Tavern. The Springhouse Café provides three meals daily, including superb buffet selections.

ABOVE: *A lazy inner-tube route snakes through the resort, mimicking a winding Hill Country stream.*

AT A GLANCE: *442 rooms with golf course view, some with private balcony; 58 suites with golf course view, some with spa tub. 3 restaurants, cooking courses, fitness center, spa, sauna, Jacuzzi, beauty salon, shops, supervised children's programs, outdoor (heated) pool, day/night tennis, golf, bicycling, nature walking, inner-tubing. NEARBY: movie theaters, hiking, horseback riding, hot-air ballooning, fishing, sailing.*

Wild Mixed-Green Salad

Raspberry Vinaigrette (yields about 5 cups):

½ tablespoon chopped shallot

½ tablespoon chopped garlic

7 ounces red wine vinegar

½ cup raspberry sauce (½ cup raspberries and ½ cup raspberry vinegar, blended)

3 cups olive oil

Salad:

12 ounces wild mixed greens

24 goat cheese medallions

All-purpose flour

Egg whites

Black and white sesame seeds

40 grapefruit sections

40 orange sections

Prepare the vinaigrette. Put the shallot and the garlic in a mixing bowl. Add the vinegar and the raspberry sauce. Mix. Pour the oil in slowly, while whisking vigorously.

Prepare the salad. Place 1½ ounces of greens in the center of each plate.

Brush the cheese medallions with the flour, then with the egg whites. Coat with the sesame seeds and deep fry. Place 3 medallions around the mixed greens on each plate. Place 5 orange sections and 5 grapefruit sections over the greens. Ladle the raspberry vinaigrette over all.

Yield: 8 servings

ABOVE: *The Hyatt Regency Hill Country Resort is a true Texas getaway.*

Sundance Resort

. . . .

The rugged wilderness around Mount Timpanagos drew actor-director and environmentalist Robert Redford here in the early 1960s, when he built his family home in the region.

. . . .

Provo, Utah

(800) 892-1600

$ – $$$$

mountain

In 1969, Redford opened the Sundance Resort, which today is a complex of cottages and mountain retreats set far back into the woods. Accommodations are elegantly rustic with furnishings inspired by Native American art.

The resort features several restaurants along with a cafeteria and a warming hut at the top of the ski slopes. The Foundry Grill, a sporty dining spot that serves three meals a day, features organic recipes prepared with ingredients from Sundance Farms. Menu selections include American Western dishes such as trout cooked on a rock. The nearby Owl Bar is a favorite watering hole of both vacationers and the local residents who populate the ski hills. The centerpiece of this restored 1890s establishment, which was transported to its present location from Wyoming, is a Victorian rosewood bar.

As the most secluded ski resort in the Utah Valley, Sundance is highly recommended for those vacationers whose objective is not to "see and be seen." No more than a thousand skiers are permitted on the mountain at any one time, so every skier can enjoy the alpine atmosphere without having to deal with interruptions or crowds. Snowboarding is not permitted at this resort.

Away from the slopes, Sundance is well known as an arts and recreational community. Every year, the resort hosts the internationally acclaimed Sundance Film Festival, a major venue on the independent-film circuit.

. . . .

ABOVE: *Sundance is tucked inconspicuously into its mountainside surroundings.*

AT A GLANCE: *20 rooms with fireplace, scenic view, some with private balcony/patio; 73 suites with fireplace, scenic view, private balcony/patio. 3 restaurants, cooking courses, steam room, shops, movie theaters, supervised children's programs, bicycling, hiking, nature walking, horseback riding, fishing, downhill/cross-country skiing, snowboarding, snowshoeing, dogsledding. NEARBY: fitness center, spa, sauna, whirlpool, beauty salon, indoor/outdoor (heated) pool, indoor/outdoor/night tennis, golf, rollerblading, hot-air ballooning, scuba diving, windsurfing, boating, marina, river rafting, skating, snowmobiling, sleigh rides.*

Warm Spinach Salad with Crispy Onions and Boar-Bacon Dressing

Boar-Bacon Dressing (yields 2½ cups):
½ pound boar bacon (or regular bacon), fried crisp and finely chopped
¼ cup sherry vinegar
1 teaspoon minced garlic
1 teaspoon chopped parsley
1 cup olive oil
Salt and pepper to taste

Salad:
All-purpose flour
Salt and pepper to taste
1 onion, thinly sliced
1 cup vegetable oil
2 pounds spinach, washed and steamed
1 pint baby pear or cherry tomatoes, halved

Prepare the dressing. Combine the bacon, vinegar, garlic, and parsley. Whisk in the oil slowly until it is fully incorporated. Season with salt and pepper.

Prepare the salad. Season the flour with the salt and pepper. Dredge the onion slices in the flour, then fry them in the oil until crisp. Drain on paper towels.

Toss the spinach with the dressing and arrange on each plate with the tomatoes. Top with the fried onion.

Serve with the boar-bacon dressing.

Yield: 6 servings

Chocolate Fondant with Dried-Fruit Salad and Hazelnut Ice Cream

Dried-Fruit Salad:
½ cup dried cherries
½ cup dried cranberries
½ cup dried apricots, finely diced
½ cup golden raisins
1 tablespoon sugar
1 cup orange-flavored liqueur, preferably Grand Marnier

Chocolate Fondant:
9 ounces chocolate
⅔ cup butter
7 eggs, separated
¼ cup sugar
2 tablespoons flour

Hazelnut ice cream

Prepare the dried-fruit salad. Mix all the ingredients and marinate for 8 hours or overnight.

Prepare the fondant. Preheat the oven to 450°F. Grease and flour 10 (2½-inch) ramekins.

Melt the chocolate and butter in the top of a double boiler. Remove from heat and whisk in the egg yolks.

Whip the egg whites with the sugar until soft peaks form. Fold in the chocolate mixture, then the flour. Turn into the prepared ramekins and bake for 15 – 20 minutes or until puffed up.

To serve, place the fondant over each serving of fruit salad. Top with a scoop of the ice cream.

Yield: 10 servings

Snowbird Ski and Summer Resort

Utah may not hear the words "Let the games begin" officially until the year 2002, but the Beehive State is already buzzing with preparations for the Winter Olympics, which will be headquartered in Salt Lake City.

Snowbird, Utah

(800) 453-3000 or (801) 742-2222

$$

mountain / spa

With all but one venue in place or under construction, the city is ready to receive thousands of athletes, coaches, and media representatives from around the world.

The Olympic torch will not illuminate the Utah sky for some time, but this region has long welcomed vacationers: they come to play in the mountains and valleys of the state, participating in such activities as downhill and cross-country skiing, helicopter skiing, snowmobiling, snow-shoeing, snowboarding, mountain biking, hiking, and mountain climbing.

The recipient of five hundred inches of snow annually, Snowbird offers Utah's longest ski season, stretching from mid-November through May. Groups will find 346 guest accommodations at Cliff Lodge Spa and Conference Center, as well as indoor and outdoor tennis courts, racquetball and squash courts, swimming pools, a 115-foot climbing wall, mountain biking trails, and soothing spa treatments.

All that physical activity does not go unrewarded. Snowbird boasts fine dining at The Aerie Restaurant, perched atop Cliff Lodge so that diners can enjoy spectacular mountain vistas along with a wide selection of dishes. Gourmet appetizers and entrées include sautéed scallops foie gras, lobster tail with seared soft-shelled crab, sea scallops, Utah lamb marinated in rosemary olive oil, and tournedos of beef and veal.

AT A GLANCE: *Cliff Lodge has 299 rooms and 47 suites; The Lodge at Snowbird has 143 rooms; The Iron Blosam has 159 units; The Inn has 40 units; some accommodations have hot tub, fireplace, kitchen, private balcony, mountain / canyon view. 9 restaurants, cooking courses, fitness center, spa, steam room, sauna, whirlpool, hot tub, beauty salon, shops, film screenings, supervised children's programs (including fishing), outdoor (heated) pool, bicycling, rollerblading, hiking, nature walking, downhill skiing, snowboarding, skating, snowshoeing, lugeing, evening sleigh rides.* NEARBY: *indoor / outdoor / night tennis, golf, cross-country skiing.*

ABOVE: *An aerial tram whisks visitors up the slopes year round.*

Smoked Chicken and Black Bean Soup

1 whole smoked chicken
1 tablespoon olive oil
1 onion, diced
1 tablespoon chopped garlic
1 green bell pepper, seeded and diced
½ tablespoon dried oregano
2 cups diced tomatoes (canned)
1½ quarts half-and-half
6 (12-ounce) cans black beans, with
    liquid
2 cups water
5 chicken bouillon cubes
½ bunch cilantro, chopped, plus
    8 sprigs
1 tablespoon liquid smoke
Tabasco to taste
Salt and pepper to taste
Tortilla chips (optional)

Cut the meat from the chicken into pieces of a desired size.

Heat the oil in a large soup pot and briefly sauté the onion, garlic, and bell pepper. Add the chicken and the oregano and continue to sauté. Add the tomato, half-and-half, beans with liquid, water, chicken bouillon cubes, cilantro, liquid smoke, and Tabasco. Simmer over low heat for 35 – 45 minutes, stirring frequently. Season with salt and pepper.

Serve garnished with the sprigs of cilantro, and tortilla chips if desired.

Yield: 8 servings

• • • • • • • • •
BELOW: *Cliff Lodge serves as home base for many vacationers during their stay at Snowbird.*

The Inn at Semi-Ah-Moo

*T*he Inn at Semi-Ah-Moo has the distinction of being the most northwesterly point in the continental United States. At this resort the slow flow of the tide sets the mood for the day.

Blaine, Washington

(800) 770-7992

$ – $$$

beach / golf / spa

Vacationers can enjoy no less than five miles of beachfront on a scenic peninsula of Puget Sound. The views of nearby peaks and verdant forests will calm any weary traveler, and if that doesn't do it a little walking through some of the eleven hundred acres of wildlife preserve will.

Even the activities at The Inn, a drive of just under two hours from Seattle, are calming. Many guests find serenity in the links of the Semi-Ah-Moo Golf Course, designed by Arnold Palmer. Players can swing away their cares on bentgrass fairways, or avail themselves of the services of the golf academy. For other guests, a boat tour to the San Juan islands or a day of spa treatments is a sybaritic pleasure. Semi-Ah-Moo offers more than three dozen treatments and services designed to soothe and restore.

Dining at this resort is no less pleasant an experience. The Pierside Restaurant is the spot for gourmet pizza and pasta with a view of Drayton Harbor. The main restaurant, Stars, features its own signature dishes such as alder plank-roasted salmon, filet mignon with Cabernet demi-glace and blue cheese beurre blanc, and roasted Ellensburg lamb with mint-jalapeño pesto.

ABOVE: *The challenging links were designed by Arnold Palmer.*

AT A GLANCE: *182 rooms and 16 suites, all with fireplace, private balcony / patio, scenic view. 3 restaurants, fitness center, spa, steam room, sauna, whirlpool, beauty salon, shops, movie theaters, supervised children's programs, indoor / outdoor (heated) pool, indoor / outdoor / night tennis, golf, bicycling, rollerblading, hiking, nature walking, horseback riding, beach, scuba diving, snorkeling, windsurfing, boating, marina, fishing.* NEARBY: *downhill / cross-country skiing, snowboarding, snowshoeing, snowmobiling.*

Apple and Lobster Soup

Lobster Stock (yields 2⅓ quarts):
1 cup butter
½ cup chopped onion
½ cup chopped celery
½ cup chopped carrot
4 sprigs of parsley
2 sprigs of thyme
1 bay leaf
2 tablespoons paprika
1 tablespoon black peppercorns
¾ pound shrimp shells
½ pound lobster tail shells
3 ounces butter, melted
½ cup all-purpose flour
5 ounces brandy
3 Roma tomatoes
2 gallons water

Soup:
1½ pounds lobster tails
Lemon juice
½ cup diced onion
⅓ tablespoon minced garlic
Sesame oil
½ teaspoon ground cinnamon
Pinch of ground cloves
¼ teaspoon ground turmeric
Pinch of ground cumin
5 cups lobster stock
1 cup whipping cream
¾ tablespoon minced ginger
1 teaspoon honey
1 Granny Smith apple, sliced
¾ sweet apple, sliced
½ teaspoon Tabasco
¾ cup Napa cabbage
⅛ cup julienned yellow bell pepper

Prepare the lobster stock. Melt the butter but do not brown. Sauté the onion, celery, carrot, parsley, thyme, bay leaf, paprika, and peppercorns until soft. Add the shells, stirring until they begin to turn red. Cook

the butter and flour over low heat to make a roux and slowly add this to the stock, stirring constantly, until the mixture is thick and free of lumps. Add the brandy and burn off the alcohol. Add the tomatoes and water and bring to a boil. Reduce heat and simmer for 40 – 45 minutes. Remove from heat and strain. Remove 5 cups of stock and reserve for the soup. Refrigerate the remainder for future use. Return the 5 cups to heat and reduce to 3 cups.

Prepare the soup. Steam or boil the lobster tails in water with some lemon juice. Remove the meat from the shell.

Sauté the onion and garlic in the oil until transparent. Add the cinnamon, cloves, turmeric, and cumin.

Bring the reserved 3 cups of lobster stock to a boil. Reduce to a simmer, add the onion mixture, and cook for 10 minutes. Strain. Return to the stove and add the cream. Simmer for 2 – 3 minutes.

Sauté the ginger in more of the oil to which the honey has been added. Add the apple and sauté until soft but firm; do not overcook. Add this to the soup.

Slice 6 small medallions from each lobster tail (making 12). Chop the remainder and add to the soup.

To serve, season each bowl with a dash of Tabasco. Pour in the soup. Divide the cabbage among the bowls, tucked along one side. Garnish with a lobster medallion, resting on the cabbage and the bell pepper julienne.

Yield: 6 servings

The American Club

The American Club bills itself "a place for all seasons." It is also a resort for all interests. Whether your passion is history or fitness, golf or nature, tennis or trap shooting, you'll find it at this resort located an hour's drive north of Milwaukee.

Kohler, Wisconsin

(800) 344-2838 or (414) 457-8000

$ – $$$$

golf / spa

Often named the Midwest's top resort destination, and the only AAA Five Diamond resort in this part of the country, the American Club has a rich history. Built in 1918 as a rooming house for Kohler Company immigrant workers, the building has always been noted for its unusual construction. The Tudor-style structure originally had 115 bedrooms, lounge, card room, bowling alley, and reading rooms. Walter Kohler had a very obvious reason for naming it the American Club: "Besides providing suitable living conditions," the club was to "be an influence in the Americanization of the foreign born and serve as a stimulus for greater love of country and a desire for higher citizenship."

As time went on, the American Club was transformed from workers' residence to public inn, hosting such notables as Admiral Richard Byrd, poet Carl Sandburg, and actress Mary Martin. Today, several refurbishments later, it retains the spirit of Kohler's 1918 building, with antique furnishings and reproductions of the original chandeliers.

Today's guests are welcomed into an expanded hotel that includes both the early residence and two new wings that preserve the integrity of the original structure. The restaurants in this resort are as outstanding as the building in which they are housed. The superb Immigrant Restaurant and Winery (open for dinner only, Tuesday through Saturday) is a series of six rooms that reflect the Wisconsin settler heritage. It features international cuisine and fine wines.

ABOVE: The Tudor-style inn was once a residence for immigrant workers.

AT A GLANCE: *215 rooms with whirlpool, some with garden view; 21 suites with whirlpool, some with garden view, 2 with fireplace. 7 restaurants.* NEARBY: *cooking courses, fitness center, spa, steam room, sauna, beauty salon, shops, movie theaters, supervised children's programs, indoor pool, indoor / outdoor tennis, golf, bicycling, rollerblading, hiking, nature walking, horseback riding, beach, lake swimming, paddle-boating, canoeing, marina, fishing, hunting, cross-country skiing, skating, snowshoeing, snowmobiling, sleigh rides.*

Rustic Apple Cake

American Club pastry chef Richard Palm dusts this cake with confectioners' sugar just before serving.

2 eggs
1¼ cups brown sugar
½ cup vegetable oil
1 teaspoon vanilla
5 medium apples (see note), peeled, cored, and chopped (3 generous cups)
1¾ cups whole wheat flour
1 teaspoon baking soda
½ teaspoon sea salt
½ teaspoon ground cinnamon
½ teaspoon grated nutmeg
Confectioners' sugar (optional)

Preheat the oven to 350°F. Grease and flour a 10-inch springform pan.

Using an electric mixer with a whip attachment, mix the eggs and sugar until pale, thick, and soufflé-like. While continuing to mix, add the oil in a thin, steady stream. Mix in the vanilla. Add the apple and stir with a spatula until the apple is coated.

Combine the flour, baking soda, salt, cinnamon, and nutmeg. Mix this into the apple mixture.

Turn the batter into the prepared pan and bake for 35 – 45 minutes or until a toothpick inserted in the center comes out clean.

Serve warm or cold, dusted with confectioners' sugar, if desired.

Note: Avoid using McIntosh apples in this recipe — a better consistency will be reached with a good baking apple. The American Club recommends Blushing Golden or Northern Spy.

Yield: 12 servings

. . . .
ABOVE: *Rustic apple cake is an American Club favorite.*

Spring Creek Resort

Winter means migration at Jackson Hole. And that means mule deer — herds of them travel to the region and forage in a landscape dotted with aspen and sagebrush.

Jackson Hole, Wyoming

(800) 443-6139

$$ – $$$

mountain

Many of those migrators travel to Spring Creek Resort, a registered wildlife preserve that offers sanctuary for both two- and four-legged visitors. At this resort, guests find a rugged Western atmosphere that contrasts with modern, first-class accommodations featuring handmade pine furniture, attentive service, and fine dining.

In the winter months, Spring Creek Resort is a wonderland of white with all the accompanying cold-weather sports at nearby venues: skating, downhill and cross-country skiing, dogsledding, ice climbing, ice fishing, sleigh rides, and even snow-mobiling out to the Old Faithful geyser. When summer brings a gentle bloom to the valley, vacationers pursue outdoor fun in the form of fly fishing on the Snake River, white-water rafting, mountain bicycling, hot-air ballooning, and just enjoying the magnificent scenery. Spring Creek guests can unwind with a luxurious soak in the spa or the outdoor hot tub complete with waterfall.

The Granary serves American cuisine featuring such specialties as medallions of elk with crushed black peppercorns and golden trout with pistachio, lemon, and parsley butter, accompanied by wines from an extensive list.

AT A GLANCE: *36 rooms, 32 suites, 32 studio apartments, 21 condos, and 3 houses, all with fireplace, private balcony, mountain view. Restaurant, hot tub, shops.* NEARBY: *outdoor (heated) pool, tennis, golf, bicycling, hiking, nature walking, horseback riding, river rafting, fishing, hunting, downhill / cross-country skiing, snowboarding, skating, snowshoeing, snowmobiling, dogsledding, sleigh rides.*

ABOVE: *Spring Creek Resort offers dramatic vistas.*

Tenderloin of Elk with Sweet Potato, Red Cabbage, Swiss Chard, and Gingerbread Sauce

Sweet Potato Cakes (yields 4 cakes):

4 sweet potatoes, peeled and sliced, lengthwise, ¼-inch thick

2 Idaho potatoes, peeled and sliced, lengthwise, ¼-inch thick

1 Granny Smith apple, peeled, cored, and thinly sliced

½ cup whipping cream

¼ cup grated Reggiano Parmesan cheese

3 eggs

1 tablespoon minced shallot

½ tablespoon finely chopped parsley

Grated nutmeg to taste

Salt and white pepper to taste

Braised Red Cabbage:

1 tablespoon butter

½ red onion, finely julienned

½ medium red cabbage, sliced paper thin

1 tablespoon brown sugar

¼ cup dry red wine

2 cups chicken stock

Pinch of ground cloves

Elk:

1 tablespoon canola oil

1½ pounds elk tenderloin (or pork loin rubbed with ground caraway seed prior to browning)

Swiss Chard:

½ pound Swiss chard or spinach

Butter

Salt and white pepper

Gingerbread Sauce:

10 ounces veal brown sauce or red wine sauce

1 (2-ounce) gingerbread cookie

Prepare the sweet potato cakes. Preheat the oven to 350°F. Grease a baking sheet with ½-inch sides. In a stainless steel bowl, mix all the ingredients. Spread the mixture on the prepared baking sheet and bake for 40 minutes or until firm. Cool. Using a cookie cutter, cut 2½-inch circles out of the potato.

Prepare the cabbage. Heat the butter in a saucepan over medium-high heat and sauté the onion until transparent. Add the cabbage and sauté until medium-soft. Dust with the sugar, then mix. Add the wine and reduce by half. Stir in the stock. Simmer until the cabbage is soft and the liquid has been absorbed. Stir in the cloves.

Prepare the elk. Preheat the oven to 350°F. Heat the oil in a sauté pan over high heat and brown the elk evenly. Transfer to a roasting pan with a rack and roast medium-rare (12 minutes) or to taste.

Prepare the Swiss chard. Heat it in enough butter to soften the chard. Season.

Prepare the gingerbread sauce. Heat the brown sauce over medium heat. Crumble the cookie into it and simmer for 5 minutes (the cookie will thicken and flavor the sauce). Strain.

To assemble, place a potato cake in the center of each plate. Using the cookie cutter as a guide, place the hot cabbage on top of the potato, filling to the rim of the cookie cutter to form a circle. The result is a two-layer circle: potato on bottom, cabbage on top. Place the hot chard on top, allowing a ¼- or ½-inch edge of the potato to show. Use the hot gingerbread sauce to evenly coat the plate around the circle. Cut the meat into 16 slices and arrange 4 slices around the potato on each plate.

Yield: 4 servings

CARIBBEAN AND MEXICO

MEXICO

CARIBBEAN

Florida (U.S.)

Grand Bahama

Great Abaco

THE BAHAMAS

Atlantic Ocean

Gulf of Mexico

Miami

Eleuthera

Cat Island

San Salvador

Nassau/ Paradise Island

Mayaguana

TURKS AND CAICOS

Cancún

Isla de Cozumel

CUBA

Great Inagua

Mexico City

Grand Cayman

JAMAICA

HAITI

DOM. REPUBLIC

St. Thomas (USVI)

Anguilla

St. Martin

Acapulco

BELIZE

Puerto Rico

St. Croix

Tortola (BVI)

St. Kitts and Nevis

ANTIGUA

Montserrat

Guadeloupe

HONDURAS

Caribbean Sea

DOMINICA

Martinique

ST. LUCIA

NICARAGUA

Aruba

Curaçao

BARBADOS

GRENADA

TRINIDAD

PANAMA

Caracas

TOBAGO

COSTA RICA

COLOMBIA

VENEZUELA

Cap Juluca

Combine the beauty of a Caribbean island known for its powder-soft beaches with Moroccan-inspired architecture featuring stark white villas. The result is an island of sensuous delights.

Maundays Bay, Anguilla

(800) 323-0139

$$$$

beach

Cap Juluca, named for the native Arawak Indian Rainbow God of Anguilla, offers a getaway for those who value privacy and indulgent service. Anguilla is reached only by ferry or plane from nearby St. Martin or San Juan, its relative inaccessibility adding to the sense of seclusion at this exclusive resort.

Cap Juluca's guests keep coming back — this resort enjoys a 50 percent return rate — and they've come to expect the attention to service that only a first-class facility can provide. They are also attracted to the blurring of the boundaries, at Cap Juluca, between indoors and out: walls of glass lead the eye to the azure waters beyond the pristine beach.

Fine dining is part of the Cap Juluca experience. Eclipse at Pimms, its main restaurant, serves California-Provençale cuisine using fresh fish and local produce. Serge Falesitch, executive chef and co-owner of Eclipse at Pimms, is also executive chef and part-owner of Eclipse in West Hollywood and former executive chef at Spago. His partner at Cap Juluca is Bernard Erpicum, formerly of Ma Maison and co-owner of Eclipse in West Hollywood. Erpicum is head chef at Cap Juluca. These two culinary leading lights bring to Anguilla a unique and striking cuisine. Their specialties include grilled peppered yellowfin tuna with artichokes, sun-dried tomato and olive vinaigrette, baby snapper with tomato, black olive, fennel, and basil vinaigrette, and wild rice and white corn risotto with grilled quail.

ABOVE: This exclusive getaway is for those who take a little pampering with their privacy.

AT A GLANCE: *58 rooms and 7 suites, all with private balcony / patio, ocean view; 6 pool villas. 2 restaurants, fitness center, supervised children's programs (seasonal), outdoor pool, day / night tennis, croquet, beach, snorkeling, windsurfing, boating, water-skiing.* NEARBY: *beauty salon, movie theaters, bicycling, hiking, nature walking, scuba diving, marina, fishing.*

Snapper Chinoise

8 ounces blanched sliced cabbage

1 cup blanched raisins

1 cup blanched whole almonds, skin removed

6 (6 – 8-ounce) red snapper fillets, skin on

6 tablespoons sesame oil

¼ cup diced tomato

½ cup julienned green onion

½ cup julienned leeks

½ cup julienned carrots

½ cup julienned ginger

6 tablespoons soy sauce

6 sprigs of chervil

Mix the blanched cabbage, raisins, and almonds. Keep warm.

In a steamer, steam the snapper for 8 – 10 minutes or until just cooked.

In a saucepan, heat the oil until it begins to smoke.

Arrange the cabbage mixture on each plate. Top with the snapper. Sprinkle the tomato around the fish. Place the onion, leek, carrot, and ginger on top of the fish. Sprinkle with the soy sauce. Pour the smoking sesame oil over the julienned vegetables. Garnish with the chervil and serve hot.

Yield: 6 servings

Creole Fish Soup

4 medium onions, chopped

4 garlic bulbs, chopped

¾ cup olive oil

2 medium Irish potatoes (see note), chopped

4 medium carrots, chopped

3 medium ripe tomatoes, chopped

Chopped fresh herbs (such as thyme, tarragon, and bay leaf) to taste

3 – 4 cups tomato paste

6 – 8 pounds fish bones or small whole fish

1½ gallons water

6 tablespoons powdered fish base

2 teaspoons Tabasco

2 teaspoons ground black pepper

¼ cup Pernod

Salt to taste

In a stock pot, sauté the onion and garlic in the oil. Add the potato, carrot, tomato, herbs, tomato paste, and fish bones and simmer for 5 – 10 minutes, stirring constantly. Add the water, fish base, Tabasco, and pepper and simmer over low heat for 60 minutes. Pass through a food mill, then return to a slow boil. Add the Pernod and season with salt and pepper. Serve hot.

Note: Ironically, the Irish potato originates in South America. It is a round, white, thin-skinned potato good for boiling, frying, and pan-roasting.

Yield: 10 servings

. . . .
BELOW: *The line between indoors and outdoors can become rather fuzzy at Cap Juluca.*

Compass Point

Compass Point guests wind down their day looking out to sea from a rocking chair on their private porch, then sleep beneath a ceiling fan in a hand-made bed covered with a Bahamian batik spread.

Nassau, Bahamas

(800) OUTPOST

$ – $$

beach

You won't find many resorts that list "state-of-the-art recording studio" among their features. But Chris Blackwell, founder of Island Records, owns a string of small, fine hotels in Caribbean countries, including Harbour Island and Compass Point, Bahamas.

Located a 25-minute drive west of Nassau, Compass Point is far removed from the frenetic pace of the casinos and mega-resorts of Cable Beach. It sits on a quiet stretch of the island near the upscale, no-visitors-allowed compound of Lyford Cay, where stars such as Sean Connery and Mick Jagger maintain residences. (Guests here might well spot a famous face, however. Compass Point has a dock for Lyford Cay residents who cruise up to its restaurant for an evening out.)

Compass Point has just 18 guest units, but this rainbow property is hard to miss with its vibrant purples, blues, yellows, and reds — the colors of the Junkanoo festival. Each unit is decorated in a style that might be described as Caribbean kitsch meets *Gilligan's Island*. Guests can choose from five oceanfront cabana rooms, which are the only air-conditioned accommodations at Compass Point, or the larger, more private huts and cottages, which feature a downstairs open-air kitchen and a picnic-table dining room.

After a day on the beach, vacationers tuck into a dinner prepared by chef Richard Haja, who specializes in California-Caribbean cuisine. The Compass Point restaurant is a casual but smart eating establishment that's popular with local residents as well as guests of the hotel.

ABOVE: Guest accommodations are located mere steps from the turquoise sea.

AT A GLANCE: *13 huts and cottages and 5 studio cabanas, all with private balcony, ocean view. Restaurant, outdoor pool, beach, watersports.* NEARBY: *shops, golf, nature walking, scuba diving, snorkeling, boating, marina, fishing, casinos.*

Conch Chowder

Compass Point chef Richard Haja says this conch chowder is "better the second day and still better the third."

¼ cup canola oil

4 conchs, finely chopped (see note)

3 bay leaves

1 sprig of thyme

1 teaspoon crushed black pepper

¼ hot chili, preferably Scotch bonnet, seeded and finely chopped

1 large onion, coarsely chopped

1 large carrot, coarsely chopped

1 large potato, coarsely chopped

1 celery stalk, coarsely chopped

1 red bell pepper, seeded and coarsely chopped

2 tablespoons dark rum

8 cups fish stock or water

5 tablespoons butter

5 tablespoons all-purpose flour

Salt

Heat the oil in a large pot. Add the conch, bay leaves, thyme, black pepper, and chili and cook for 5 – 7 minutes, stirring constantly. Add the onion, carrot, potato, celery, and bell pepper and cook for another 5 minutes. Add the rum and the stock. Bring to a boil and simmer for 10 minutes.

Meanwhile, make a roux by melting the butter over medium heat and whisking in the flour. Cook, whisking constantly, until golden to brown in color. Remove from heat and let cool. Whisk the roux into the chowder and simmer for 30 minutes over very low heat. Add salt to taste. Remove the bay leaves and the sprig of thyme, then serve immediately.

Note: The conch is a mollusk of the abalone and snail family. At its peak, in summer, fresh conch is available in Chinese and Italian markets or specialty fish markets. It is also available frozen.

Yield: 4 servings

· · · · · · · · · ·

BELOW: *A row of guest bungalows as colorful as a box of crayons contrasts with the stark white of the sandy beach.*

Atlantis, Paradise Island

*T*he vacationers look up through the sea water, the sun filtering down in liquid shafts and illuminating the hundreds of fish around them. Suddenly, ominously, the light is blocked by a great, looming shadow — a shark!

*Paradise Island,
Bahamas*

(800) 321-3000

$$

beach

Directly overhead, the six-foot predator swims slowly, deliberately, sending schools of yellow grunts scurrying for shelter.

The vacationers, however, unlike the schools of fish and the large, spiny lobster on the sandy floor below, are not worried. The tourists in the hundred-foot-long clear tunnel simply delight in the view. Surrounded by sharks, manta rays, sea turtles, and thousands of tropical fish in the world's largest open-air aquarium, they are experiencing the thrill of scuba diving without ever getting wet.

The tunnel and the 14-acre water gardens that surround it are features of the Atlantis, Paradise Island. The lavish resort, refurbished from a former property, is one of the most extravagant in the Caribbean. And it's going to be bigger and better, with an additional casino and twelve hundred new guest rooms.

For all its features, though, the hotel is just a backdrop for the 14-acre waterscape, where more than 40 waterfalls splash and churn sea water into fish-filled lagoons that weave through walkways, bridges, and open-air bars. The huge observation tanks are constructed of man-made stone and coral formations to simulate a marine environment. Guests flock to the Predator Lagoon for a close-up view of the half dozen reef sharks that swim alongside barracudas and rays.

Atlantis, Paradise Island features a range of restaurants: The Bahamian Club steakhouse, The Boat House Grill (where steaks and seafood are prepared on tableside grills), Mama Loo's Chinese restaurant, The Water's Edge, and Villa d'Este, a trattoria specializing in Northern Italian cuisine. Café Martinique, a romantic French restaurant situated at water's edge, was featured in the James Bond movie *Thunderball*. It offers Bahamian dishes such as sautéed grouper with slivered almonds, as well as French cuisine.

ABOVE: *This resort is a waterscape, with rides, waterfalls, and fish-filled lagoons.*

AT A GLANCE: *1,082 rooms and 62 suites, all with private balcony. 12 restaurants, fitness center, beauty salon, shops, outdoor pool, nature walking, beach, watersports, snorkeling, fish feeding.* NEARBY: *day / night tennis, golf, scuba diving, windsurfing, fishing.*

Caribbean Seafood Strudel with Mango-Lime Sauce

Seafood Strudel:

Olive oil

½ pound grouper

8 large shrimp, peeled and deveined

⅓ pound scallops

1 lobster tail

Salt and pepper to taste

1 onion, sliced

Shrimp and lobster shells

1 tablespoon tomato paste

1 cup sherry

2 cups whipping cream

¼ cup julienned basil

½ cup grated Parmesan cheese

½ cup bread crumbs

6 sheets phyllo dough layered with melted butter

Mango-Lime Sauce:

2 mangoes, peeled, pitted, and diced

1 cup pineapple juice

¼ cup lime juice (or to taste)

Prepare the seafood strudel. In a very hot pan with the oil, separately sear the grouper, shrimp, scallops, and lobster tail, seasoned with salt and pepper. Cool and drain, then dice.

Sauté the onion and shrimp and lobster shells in oil. Add the tomato paste and sherry. Cover and reduce by half. Add the cream and reduce until thickened. Strain the mixture over the diced seafood. Add the basil, cheese, and bread crumbs. Cool.

Preheat the oven to 375°F. Place the seafood mixture on the phyllo sheets and roll into a log. Fold the ends so the mixture cannot leak out. Bake on parchment paper for 15 minutes or until browned.

Prepare the mango-lime sauce. Bring all the ingredients to a boil. Strain.

Slice the seafood strudel and serve with the mango-lime sauce.

Yield: 4 servings

· · · · · · · · · · ·

BELOW: *Guests of the Atlantis, Paradise Island enter an undersea world of sharks, sea turtles, and rays.*

Sugar Mill Hotel

*T*he Sugar Mill, one of the finest small hotels in the Caribbean, offers guests an opportunity to enjoy a spectacular setting while at the same time feeling they are participating in island life.

*Tortola,
British Virgin
Islands*

*(800) 462-8834 or
(800) 209-6874*

$$ – $$$

beach

This inn is located on the site of the Appleby Plantation, which flourished in the days of sugar and slaves. The only remnants of the original buildings are the ruins of the 340-year-old stone sugar mill, which today form part of the hotel's romantic candlelit restaurant — its stone walls forming a backdrop for Haitian artwork. Another reminder of the inn's past is the circular swimming pool: it is built on the site of a treadmill where oxen powered the machinery that crushed the sugar cane to make rum.

Many gourmands are familiar with the work of Jinx and Jeff Morgan, the Sugar Mill's owners. These cookbook authors and *Bon Appetit* columnists are well known in the world of fine food. The recipe for happiness for this former California couple included not only writing about food, but sharing the gourmet experience in a tropical environment. Since the Morgans began operating the resort in 1982, the Sugar Mill Hotel has been a prime destination for those vacationers who seek tranquility and privacy.

The restaurant menu changes daily. A typical dinner might begin with smoked conch pâté or smoked scallops and then proceed to roasted corn soup or West Indian tania soup. Entrées range from tropical game hen with orange-curry butter, to fresh fish in banana leaves with herb butter, to roasted pepper-stuffed pork tenderloin with pineapple chipotle sauce. Diners at this resort can take home more than their memories: in 1997 the Morgans published *The Sugar Mill Caribbean Cookbook* (Harvard Common Press), which includes such dishes as scallops in puff pastry with roasted red pepper sauce (see recipe opposite).

ABOVE: *The circular swimming pool: where oxen were used to crush sugar cane.*

AT A GLANCE: *16 rooms, 4 suites, and 1 villa, all with private balcony, ocean view. 2 restaurants, outdoor pool, beach, watersports, snorkeling, fishing.* NEARBY: *fitness center, spa, beauty salon, shops, movie theaters, day / night tennis, bicycling, hiking, nature walking, horseback riding, scuba diving, windsurfing, boating, marina.*

Scallops in Puff Pastry with Roasted Red Pepper Sauce

The Sugar Mill Hotel uses a real scallop shell as a template to cut out the pastry. An alternative, says the chef, is to draw a shell on paper and then cut it out to use as a guide.

Roasted Red Pepper Sauce:
2 red bell peppers, or 3 pimentos
3 tablespoons minced onion
1 cup dry white wine
½ cup clam broth
½ cup water
2 cups whipping cream
2 tablespoons lemon juice
Salt and pepper
Commercial puff pastry

Scallops:
2½ pounds scallops
½ bay leaf
Pinch of thyme
¼ teaspoon salt
1 cup dry white wine
2 tablespoons cold butter

Prepare the roasted red pepper sauce. If using fresh peppers, roast, peel, and seed (see note on page 85). Slice the peppers.

Boil the bell pepper, onion, wine, broth, and water in a heavy pan until the liquid is reduced to about 3 tablespoons. Add the cream and simmer until thick. In a blender or food processor, whirl until smooth. Season with the lemon juice and salt and pepper. Reserve.

Cut six scallop-shell shapes from the puff pastry and bake, according to the directions on the package, until puffed up and golden brown. Split in half horizontally. Keep warm.

Prepare the scallops. In a saucepan, bring to the boiling point the scallops, bay leaf, thyme, salt, wine, and enough water to cover. Immediately lower the heat and poach, covered, in barely simmering water for 3 – 4 minutes or until the scallops are tender (boiling will make them tough). Drain the scallops.

Fill the pastry shells with the scallops. Reheat the sauce, stir the butter into it, and spoon some of the sauce over the scallops. Serve immediately.

Yield: 6 servings

· · · · · · · · · ·

BELOW: *Caribbean ingredients meet California cuisine in an imaginative Sugar Mill menu that changes daily.*

Sonesta Beach Resort & Casino Curaçao

The Sonesta is a veritable oasis on this arid island. Guests can relax poolside beneath stately palms or sit on their terrace and enjoy a show of birds delighting in the tropical foliage.

Willemstad, Curaçao

(800) 766-3782

$$

beach

This elegant resort is ideally situated: it stretches along a wide swath of beach just a short ride from both the airport and the city.

The architecture of the Sonesta is in the style of the Netherlands Antilles. Cool, lemon-colored walls contrast with roofs the color of chili peppers.

Especially appealing is the low-rise, open-air quality of this resort. Upon arrival, Sonesta guests are greeted with a view over a cascading fountain across the palm-shaded pool and the sea beyond. Every room features either a balcony or a patio — ground-floor rooms have direct access to the beach — and at least a partial ocean view.

Diners have several options. The sophisticated Emerald Bar and Grille features grilled fish, steak, and poultry just steps from the casino and the main lobby. For the ultimate in evening romance, Portofino serves Northern Italian delicacies under the stars.

Built in 1992, this resort reflects the atmosphere of Curaçao, an island tucked into the southern reaches of the Caribbean less than 40 miles from the coast of South America. Most Sonesta staff members, like many residents of Curaçao, speak an amazing total of five languages: Dutch, Spanish, English, either French or German, and Papiamento. Papiamento, the language spoken on the streets of Curaçao, is a veritable cocktail of tongues. Spanish, Portuguese, French, Dutch, Indian, English, and some African dialects combine to form the *lingua franca* of the Netherlands Antilles. While Dutch is the official language of Curaçao, and a great number of its visitors are Dutch-speaking, many of its tourists are Spanish-speaking vacationers from South America.

ABOVE: *The lemon-tinted buildings reflect the traditional architecture of Curaçao.*

AT A GLANCE: *214 rooms and 34 suites, all with private balcony/patio. 3 restaurants, fitness center, steam room, sauna, whirlpool, shops, supervised children's programs, outdoor pool, day/night tennis, beach, scuba diving, snorkeling, ocean kayaking, banana boat rides, tube rides, wave runners.* NEARBY: *beauty salon, movie theaters, golf, bicycling, hiking, nature walking, horseback riding, boating, marina, fishing.*

Keshi Yena
(Stuffed Edam Cheese)

1 (2 – 2½-pound) wheel of Edam
    cheese
Butter, margarine, or oil
3 tomatoes, peeled and chopped
2 onions, sliced
1 small garlic clove, chopped
1 green bell pepper, seeded and
    chopped
¼ cup sliced olives
1 tablespoon capers
1 tablespoon chopped parsley
¼ hot chili, minced, or Tabasco to taste
2 teaspoons Worcestershire sauce
1 tablespoon tomato paste
2 tablespoons ketchup
2 tablespoons piccalilli relish
½ cup raisins and chopped prunes,
    mixed
Salt and pepper to taste
2 pounds tuna or salmon fillets,
    chopped or finely diced (see note)
4 eggs, beaten, plus 1 egg, beaten

Prepare the cheese according to either the following instructions or the alternative method provided at the bottom of this recipe.

Cut a circle on the top of the cheese wheel. Scoop out the cheese, leaving a shell ¼ – ½-inch thick. Reserve the lid.

Heat the butter and sauté all the ingredients except the eggs. Simmer for 20 minutes or until the tomato is reduced. Blend in the 4 beaten eggs.

Fill the cheese with the vegetable mixture and replace the cheese lid. Brush the remaining 1 beaten egg on top of the cheese as a sealant.

Grease a casserole or the top of a double boiler. If a casserole, set in a pan of hot water and place in a 350°F oven for 90 minutes; if

a double boiler, cover and place over simmering water for 90 minutes.

Cut into wedges and serve as a main dish with rice or potatoes.

Alternative method of cheese preparation: Cut the cheese into ¼-inch slices. Butter a large, deep dish or individual custard cups and line with half the cheese slices, overlapping the edges. Add the vegetable and egg mixture, then the rest of the cheese. Brush with the remaining 1 beaten egg to seal.

Note: Chicken or ground beef can be substituted for the fish.

Yield: 10 – 12 servings

. . . .
ABOVE: *Stately palms line the pool and overlook the sea adjacent to the Sonesta Beach Resort & Casino Curaçao.*

Sandals Royal Jamaican

T*he Sandals chain, which was begun in Jamaica and now also operates couples-only resorts in the Bahamas, Antigua, and St. Lucia, caters to fun-loving people who seek an active vacation.*

Montego Bay, Jamaica

(800) SANDALS

$$

beach

The Sandals Royal Jamaican is more subdued than its cousins, but what it lacks in liveliness it more than makes up for in lavishness. Special touches — cooled towels on the beach, herbal teas in the gym, aromatic saunas, Continental room service — make this resort, which is designed to resemble a Jamaican plantation, truly royal. It features magnificent grounds, mini-suites with private balconies overlooking azure waters, and public areas that blur the boundaries between indoors and outdoors.

This resort also boasts Jamaica's only offshore restaurant. Bali Hai serves Indonesian cuisine, prepared by an Indonesian chef and served in an authentic atmosphere. Guests are ferried to an island (which by day serves as a beach and a beach bar) for a multi-course meal served family-style. When each couple arrives, the hostess gives them wraps to simultaneously tie around each other's waist. It's a romantic start to a dreamy candlelight dinner in an exotic setting.

The dining policy of the Sandals chain is one of its unique features. This "Stay at One, Enjoy All Six" arrangement gives guests dining privileges at the 19 Sandals restaurants in Jamaica. Each hotel reservations desk handles bookings for the chain's many restaurants, which range from Italian to West Indian, from Japanese to Jamaican. Shuttle service to the Montego Bay area Sandals restaurants is complimentary.

Recently, Sandals has been hosting an annual Sandals Cooking Academy, a five-day cooking course that changes location each year. It features top U.S. chefs as well as Sandals' own chefs. The curriculum focuses on light and Caribbean cuisine.

ABOVE: *This deluxe resort caters to vacationing couples.*

AT A GLANCE: *190 rooms with private balcony, ocean/garden view, some with whirlpool, Jacuzzi. 4 restaurants, fitness center, spa, steam room, sauna, whirlpool, beauty salon, outdoor pool, day/night tennis, beach, scuba diving, snorkeling, windsurfing.* NEARBY: *movie theaters, golf, bicycling, rollerblading, hiking, nature walking, horseback riding; boating, fishing, and river rafting tours.*

Jerk Pork

½ cup chopped onion

½ cup chopped garlic

¼ cup chopped ginger

2 scallions

1 Scotch Bonnet chili, or to taste, seeded

1 teaspoon pimento seeds or ground allspice

1 teaspoon chopped thyme

¼ cup soy sauce

¼ cup corn oil

Salt to taste

Vinegar to taste

4 pounds pork legs

In a food processor, blend the onion, garlic, ginger, scallion, chili, pimento, thyme, soy sauce, and corn oil to a smooth paste. Mix in the salt and vinegar. Rub the paste on the pork and marinate in the refrigerator for at least 2 hours, preferably overnight.

Barbecue the pork over an open fire, turning often to avoid burning.

Yield: 12 servings

BELOW: *Guests of the Sandals Royal Jamaican have the opportunity to master a new watersport.*

Grand Lido

This posh resort is designed for those who demand the very best in service. From its marble entrance to its regal columns, the Grand Lido is a cut above your typical beachfront resort.

Negril, Jamaica

(800) GO SUPER

$$$

beach

Standard features in the all-inclusive package include 24-hour room service, direct-dial telephone, satellite TV, and manicure or pedicure. For the romantically inclined, the resort even offers complimentary weddings and vow-renewal ceremonies.

The Grand Lido, a member of the SuperClubs chain, provides daily tennis, snorkeling, scuba diving, and water-skiing lessons. For guests who just want to laze in the sun, there's a luxuriant white sandy beach.

The hotel faces the clear blue waters of Bloody Bay (named during the days when whalers cleaned their catch here), which is home to the *M. / Y. Zein*. Aristotle Onassis gave this majestic 147-foot yacht to Princess Grace as a wedding present. Today, Grand Lido guests enjoy sunset cruises and even specially arranged parties and weddings aboard the honeymoon yacht.

Three specialty restaurants, as well as a main dining room and three clubhouses, provide plenty of mealtime choices. For casual dining, guests choose Café Lido, which serves Continental cuisine, or LaPasta. The more formal Piacere requires jacket and tie — but those travelers who packed light need not worry: like everything else at the Grand Lido, this detail is discreetly provided.

ABOVE: This resort is one of the most luxurious in the Caribbean.

AT A GLANCE: *200 rooms and 218 suites, all with private balcony / patio, ocean view. 7 restaurants, fitness center, beauty salon, outdoor pool, day / night tennis, golf, bicycling, nature walking, beach, scuba diving, snorkeling, windsurfing, waterbiking, boating, kayaking, sailing, glass-bottom boat rides.*

Millefeuilles of Beef Tenderloin

Sauce:

1 cup chopped onion

4 teaspoons finely chopped garlic

¼ cup butter

2 teaspoons green peppercorns

2 teaspoons dried thyme

2 cups dried mushrooms (shiitake, porcini, morels), rehydrated, finely diced

1 cup diced carrot

1 bay leaf, broken into small pieces

Salt and pepper to taste

4 teaspoons tomato paste

4 cups dry red wine

4 cups beef stock

Beef:

4 (7-ounce) beef tenderloins

Salt and pepper to taste

½ cup olive oil

¼ cup butter

1 cup sliced onion

4 teaspoons chopped garlic

1 cup dried Chinese mushrooms (such as shiitake), rehydrated, finely diced

4 cups white button mushrooms, finely diced

4 teaspoons snipped chives

4 teaspoons chopped basil

Prepare the sauce. Sauté the onion and garlic in the butter. Add the peppercorns, thyme, mushrooms, carrot, bay leaf, salt and pepper, and tomato paste. Stir for a few minutes. Add the wine and reduce by half. Add the stock and continue to reduce until the desired consistency is reached. Strain and keep warm.

Prepare the beef. Season with salt and pepper on both sides. Heat the oil in a sauté pan and sear the meat on both sides, then remove. Add the butter to the oil and fry the onion, garlic, mushrooms, chives, and basil for 5 minutes. Set aside.

Preheat the oven to 350°F. Cut each tenderloin into three slices and place in a shallow baking dish. Cook for 10 minutes or until done.

To serve, place a slice of meat on each plate. Add some of the mushroom mixture, then the sauce. Top with a second slice of meat, the mushroom mixture, then more sauce. Add a third slice, more of the mushroom mixture, and more sauce. Serve immediately.

Yield: 4 servings

· · · · · · · · · · ·

BELOW: *Watersports, gourmet meals, room service — even weddings — are all part of the Grand Lido package.*

Hyatt Dorado Beach Resort & Casino

F or vacationers seeking comfort along with classic simplicity, the Hyatt Dorado Beach fits the bill. Its low-rise buildings overlooking a wide stretch of palm-lined beach exude a 1950s air in the finest tradition of Laurance Rockefeller's Rockresorts.

*Dorado,
Puerto Rico*

(800) 233-1234

$$ – $$$$

beach / golf

Located on the site of a former grapefruit and coconut plantation, the resort features lush grounds with towering palms and casuarina trees that dwarf the many one-storey buildings sprinkled throughout the property. This resort has a casual feel, from its Saltillo tile floors to the clean lines of its mahogany and redwood reception area.

The Su Casa restaurant, located in the 1900 hacienda that was the home of the plantation owner, serves Spanish and Caribbean dishes. Other dining options are the stylish Surf Room, the Ocean Terrace for breakfast and lunch (and dinner in high season), and the golf pro shop and golf bohio for lunch.

Like all large Puerto Rican resorts, the Hyatt Dorado Beach has something for everyone — even a windsurfing school. However, this resort is especially geared for golfers. The Dorado East and Dorado West courses have hosted World Cup Golf, the Tournament of Champions, and many other competitions. The East course is best known for its 13th hole, which Jack Nicklaus ranks as one of the top 10 holes in the world. The West course is noted for its changing directions, designed to make the ever-present sea breezes challenging to negotiate. The resort offers a tempting year-round golf package.

ABOVE: *The Su Casa restaurant serves Spanish and Caribbean cuisine in a century-old hacienda.*

AT A GLANCE: *298 rooms, most with private balcony, ocean view; 17 suites, most with ocean view; 1 casita. 4 restaurants, fitness center, spa, sauna, beauty salon, shops, outdoor pool, day / night tennis, golf, bicycling, nature walking, beach, snorkeling, windsurfing.* NEARBY: *supervised children's programs, horseback riding, scuba diving.*

Conch Fritters with Jerk Spice Rémoulade

Jerk Spice Rémoulade (yields 3 cups):

1 cup mayonnaise

2 large sour pickles, chopped

2 tablespoons water

2 tablespoons finely chopped green
   onion

1 tablespoon chopped parsley

1 teaspoon minced garlic

1 teaspoon chopped capers

1 teaspoon paprika

1 teaspoon prepared mustard

½ teaspoon powdered mustard

½ teaspoon dried tarragon

1½ teaspoons Jamaican jerk spice

½ teaspoon white pepper

Salt to taste

Conch Fritters:

1 pound finely ground conch meat (see
   note on page 131)

1 small yellow onion, finely diced

1 celery stalk, finely diced

1 small red bell pepper, finely diced

1 cup white bread crumbs

2 – 3 eggs

2 tablespoons chopped parsley

1½ teaspoons Old Bay brand spice
   (or Cajun seafood spice)

½ teaspoon cayenne

Salt to taste

All-purpose flour

Prepare the rémoulade. Gently mix all the ingredients until well blended. Refrigerate.

Prepare the fritters. Combine all the ingredients except the flour. Form the mixture into small balls. Lightly dip in the flour and deep fry until golden brown. Serve with the rémoulade.

Yield: 6 – 8 servings

. . . .

ABOVE: *The Dorado East and Dorado West courses have hosted many professional competitions.*

Four Seasons Resort Nevis

This resort is not only the most luxurious on the island of Nevis, it is one of the top resorts in the entire Caribbean area. The grounds are dotted with coconut palms and other carefully tended fauna.

Nevis,
St. Kitts and Nevis

(800) 332-3442

$$$$

beach / golf

Guests can windsurf, scuba dive, play tennis on one of 10 courts, or golf on the course designed by Robert Trent Jones, Jr. They can also take advantage of round-the-clock room service, watch movies on their VCRs or cable TV, lounge in an outdoor hot tub, or just sun themselves around the pool, cooled by Evian sprayed on guests by ever watchful attendants.

The dining at the Four Seasons Resort Nevis is as varied as its activities. The Grill Room, an open-air restaurant overlooking the sea, serves New American and Mediter-ranean cuisine at dinnertime. Upstairs in the Great House, the candlelit Dining Room offers many local seafood specialties accompanied by wines from an extensive list.

When word went out that the Four Seasons was coming to Nevis, doomsayers predicted the end of the unspoiled environment for which the island is known. But then Hurricane Hugo hit, and the Four Seasons halted construction of the hotel and put its crews to work cleaning up the island. Today, even other Nevis innkeepers sing the praises of this resort.

Columbus first named this tiny isle for the ever-present cloud that hovered over its mountain peak, giving it the appearance of being snow-capped. A cloud lingers over Mount Nevis to this very day. Home to only nine thousand people, charming Nevis is often cited as an example of the Caribbean "the way it used to be."

ABOVE: *This resort occupies a strategic spot between Mount Nevis and the sea.*

AT A GLANCE: *196 rooms and 15 suites, all with private balcony / patio, mountain / ocean / golf course view. 3 restaurants, fitness center, spa, steam room, sauna, beauty salon, shops, supervised children's programs, outdoor pool, day / night tennis, golf, bicycling, hiking, nature walking, beach, scuba diving, snorkeling, windsurfing, boating, marina, fishing.*

Saffron Potato-Crusted Grouper with Roma Tomato and Basil Salad and Snow Peas

Roma Tomato and Basil Salad:
2 tablespoons olive oil
1 tablespoon balsamic vinegar
½ teaspoon finely chopped shallot
Salt and pepper to taste
5 Roma tomatoes, quartered
6 basil leaves, julienned

Saffron Potato-Crusted Grouper:
2 potatoes, peeled
Pinch of saffron
¼ cup skim milk
Salt and pepper to taste
4 (5-ounce) grouper fillets, skin on

12 ounces snow peas

Prepare the salad. Make a vinaigrette by combining the oil, vinegar, and shallot. Season with the salt and pepper. Marinate the tomatoes with the basil in the vinaigrette for 60 minutes.

Prepare the fish. Preheat the oven to 350°F. Cook the potatoes until tender, then strain and mash. Heat the saffron in the milk, add salt and pepper, and mix with the potatoes. Pipe the crust onto the grouper fillets and bake for 8 minutes.

Blanch the snow peas.

To serve, place a grouper fillet on each plate. Surround it with the tomatoes and snow peas drizzled with any remaining vinaigrette.

Yield: 4 servings

. . . .
BELOW: *Both fine and casual dining await guests at the Four Seasons Resort Nevis.*

Montpelier Hotel & Beach Club

Montpelier Hotel & Beach Club's most famous recent guest was Princess Diana. When Diana visited Nevis with her children, she opted for the seclusion of this classic plantation inn.

Nevis,
St. Kitts and Nevis

(800) 223-9832 or
(869) 469-3462

$$

beach

Royals and honeymooners alike find peace and seclusion in this very British hotel located on the slopes of Mount Nevis.

Princess Diana focused the eyes of the world on Montpelier, but her visit hardly marked the resort's first brush with royalty. On March 11, 1787, Admiral Horatio Nelson married Fanny Nisbet before a royal audience on these very grounds. Today, it's a popular choice for everyone: recently Montpelier was named number one overall and for food, ambience, and service by readers of *Condé Nast Traveler* magazine.

The plantation includes a 16-room inn that exudes a dignified British air, much appreciated by those who travel to the Caribbean for its promise of serenity. The inn provides shuttle service to the beaches, but the mood here is designed for those who seek tranquility as well as a tan. Evenings begin with cocktails served in the Great Room — guests discuss their day as amiable owners James and Celia Gaskell take orders for dinner. Eventually diners make their way to the veranda for an al fresco meal served with grace and style. Typical dishes include fillet of mahimahi in Swiss cheese crust, breast of duck in soy and ginger, tenderloin of veal, and grilled lobster with Creole hollandaise.

Although many resorts make the claim, Montpelier Hotel & Beach Club truly is the epitome of casual elegance, and it truly does offer a taste of the Caribbean's colonial past.

This resort closes annually from late August through early October.

ABOVE: The beach club offers hours of sun and solitude.

AT A GLANCE: *16 rooms and 1 suite, all with hot tub, private patio, ocean view. Restaurant, outdoor pool, tennis, hiking, nature walking, horseback riding.* NEARBY: *golf, bicycling, beach, scuba diving, snorkeling, windsurfing, boating, fishing.*

Curried Butternut, Sweet Potato, and Cheddar Soup

1 onion, chopped

3 garlic cloves, chopped

2 celery stalks, chopped

2 leeks, chopped

½ cup olive oil

2 tablespoons curry powder

Chopped cilantro to taste

5 butternut squash, peeled and
   chopped (5 pounds)

5 sweet potatoes, peeled and chopped

4 quarts chicken stock

2 cups grated Cheddar cheese

Croutons

Salt and pepper to taste

½ cup whipping cream (optional)

Sauté the onion, garlic, celery, and leek in the oil until tender. Add the curry powder, cilantro, squash, and sweet potato. Cook over low heat for 3 – 4 minutes to soften the vegetables without letting them brown. Add the stock and bring to a boil, then simmer for 45 minutes or until the sweet potato is very soft.

Place the mixture in a blender, add the cheese, and process.

To serve, add the croutons, salt and pepper, and, if desired, a whirl of cream.

Yield: 12 servings

· · · · · · · · · ·

BELOW: *Montpelier Hotel & Beach Club combines Old World charm with New World casualness.*

Mount Nevis Hotel and Beach Club

On a tropical island whose resorts boast palm-lined beaches, historic great houses, and guest lists that include Princess Diana, it isn't easy to make your mark.

*Nevis,
St. Kitts and Nevis*

(800) 75-NEVIS

$$

beach

But the Mount Nevis Hotel and Beach Club has done it — by offering good, contemporary accommodations, spectacular views, and, most of all, gourmet dining.

The Mount Nevis Restaurant, overlooking the aquamarine waters of the Caribbean and Nevis's sister island, St. Kitts, is held in high regard in gastronomic circles. Thanks to chef Jeff DeBarbieri, this hilltop resort is now a dining choice for day visitors as well as guests of the resort. DeBarbieri, who trained with Swiss chef Gaspard Caloz at New York's Tavern on the Green, has created such specialties as lobster wontons with ginger-soy dipping sauce, grilled snapper with mango and tomatillo salsa, and island-spiced crème brûlée (see recipe opposite). "Nevis has tremendous fresh ingredients and a strong, interesting tradition of Creole cuisine," says DeBarbieri. "I try to blend these two assets to create memorable and appealing dishes."

The restaurant features magnificent vistas — of both the Caribbean Sea and towering Mount Nevis with its cloudy cap that inspired Columbus to name the island "Our Lady of the Snows." Visitors have no fear of experiencing chilly days at this latitude, however. They spend hours luxuriating in a poolside hammock, sunning themselves on powdery white sand at the beach club, or hiking on nearby trails, where, in early morning or late afternoon, it isn't uncommon to spot a vervet monkey.

ABOVE: From their lofty perch, guests of the resort can see St. Kitts in the distance.

AT A GLANCE: *32 rooms and 16 suites, all with private balcony/patio, sea/St. Kitts view. 2 restaurants, video movie library, outdoor pool, hiking, nature walking, kite flying.* NEARBY: *beauty salon, shops, tennis, golf, horseback riding, beach, scuba diving, snorkeling, windsurfing, boating, fishing.*

Coconut-Fried Lobster

Batter:

1 cup all-purpose flour

¼ cup cornstarch

Cayenne to taste

Salt and pepper to taste

1 (12-ounce) bottle of beer

Sauce:

8 tablespoons butter

2 tablespoons chopped shallot

1 cup diced ripe mango

½ cup diced peeled tomato

½ cup dry white wine

½ cup fish or chicken stock

2 tablespoons lemon or lime juice

4 tablespoons chopped cilantro

Cayenne to taste

Salt and pepper to taste

Lobster:

2 (12-ounce) lobster tails, split and
  deveined, meat removed

4 cups shredded unsweetened coconut

Prepare the batter. Combine the flour, cornstarch, cayenne, and salt and pepper. Whisk in the beer until the mixture is smooth and the consistency of thin pancake batter (all of the beer may not be required). Cover and let rest for 30 minutes.

Prepare the sauce. Place 2 tablespoons of the butter in a sauté pan and sauté the shallot for 15 seconds over medium-high heat. Add the mango and tomato and sauté for another 15 seconds. Add the wine, stock, lemon juice, and cilantro and reduce by half. Whisk in the remaining 6 tablespoons of butter. Season and remove from heat. Keep warm.

Preheat a deep fryer to 375°F. Hold the lobster by the tail shell section and dip it into the batter, letting the excess batter drip off. Dredge in the coconut until well coated.

Repeat with the other half of the lobster tail. Carefully drop the two halves into the deep fryer and fry until lightly browned and cooked through. Drain on paper towels.

Serve whole or sliced, with the sauce.

Yield: 4 servings

Island-Spiced Crème Brûlée

2¼ cups whipping cream

6 egg yolks

⅓ cup sugar

¾ teaspoon ground cinnamon

½ teaspoon ground allspice

¼ teaspoon grated nutmeg

2 tablespoons Captain Morgan
  Spiced Rum

White or brown sugar

Preheat the oven to 350°F.

Warm the cream over low heat (do not boil).

Whisk the egg yolks with the sugar and spices until blended. Add the cream and stir until well combined. Add the rum and skim the foam from the surface.

Pour into 6 (6-ounce) custard dishes. Place in a shallow pan with water reaching halfway up the sides of the dishes and bake for 20 minutes or until set. Cool at room temperature, then refrigerate.

Before serving, sprinkle with the sugar and caramelize under a broiler or with a torch.

Yield: 6 servings

Nisbet Plantation Beach Club

*T*he beautiful island of Nevis has been the playground of many British celebrities, including Princess Diana, but its greatest brush with royalty occurred on March 11, 1787.

Nevis,
St. Kitts and Nevis

(800) 742-6008

$$ – $$$$

beach

The wedding of Admiral Horatio Nelson and Nevis resident Fanny Nisbet on that date attracted a royal audience. Two centuries later, the event is still commemorated on this tiny isle.

Fanny Nisbet lived on a beachfront plantation that today is the Nisbet Plantation Beach Club. This 38-room inn boasts perhaps the Caribbean's most striking vista: a quarter-mile palm-lined walk from the Great House to one of the finest beaches in Nevis.

Guests stay in lemon-tinted bungalows and lanai suites scattered throughout the property. The premier units, which feature a spacious living room, are designed for groups of four.

Visitors can engage in snorkeling, ocean or pool swimming, tennis, or that most British of sports, croquet.

The focal point of the resort is the Great House, which dates back to the earliest days of the sugar plantation, circa 1778. This two-storey building featuring an upstairs screened veranda is home to a superb restaurant. Guests like to start their evening with a drink at the Great House bar, then step out to the veranda for a memorable meal accompanied by fine wines.

The Coconuts restaurant, which is more casual, serves lunch and a full breakfast. This might include dishes such as eggs Florentine, Nevisian saltfish with coconut johnnycake, or Caribbean toast. Continental breakfast can be brought to those who have difficulty tearing themselves away from the romance of their hideaway abode.

All room rates at the Nisbet Plantation Beach Club include breakfast and dinner.

ABOVE: *The Great House, dating back more than two centuries, is home to the resort's fine dining restaurant.*

AT A GLANCE: *16 rooms with private patio, some with ocean view; 22 suites with private balcony / patio, ocean view. 2 restaurants, outdoor pool, tennis, beach, watersports, snorkeling.* NEARBY: *fitness center, beauty salon, shops, golf, bicycling, hiking, nature walking, scuba diving, windsurfing, boating, fishing.*

Chilled Pear and Beet Soup with Ginger-Cinnamon Croutons

Chilled Pear and Beet Soup:
2 (12-ounce) beets, whole, unpeeled
3 quarts water
1 cup dry white wine
¾ cup sugar
½ cup lime juice
½ cup frozen orange juice concentrate, thawed
2 large cinnamon sticks
1 large vanilla bean, cut and scraped
4 pounds Bosc pears, peeled and scored
2 cups milk
2 cups whipping cream
½ cup Grand Marnier

Ginger-Cinnamon Croutons:
¼ cup butter
1 teaspoon finely chopped ginger
5 slices toast, cubed
1 teaspoon ground cinnamon

Prepare the soup. Wash and steam the beets until tender. Place in cold water, then rub the peel off with a paper towel. Slice the beets.

Bring to a boil the water, wine, sugar, lime juice, orange juice concentrate, cinnamon sticks, and vanilla bean. Add the pears and poach for 20 minutes or until soft. Remove the cinnamon sticks and purée the mixture, along with the beets, in a blender. Add the milk, cream, and Grand Marnier. Refrigerate.

Prepare the croutons. Heat the butter and ginger in a sauté pan. Add the bread cubes and toss until golden brown. Add the ground cinnamon. Sprinkle the croutons over the chilled soup just before serving.

Yield: 10 servings

ABOVE: *At the Nisbet Plantation Beach Club, a former sugar mill is tucked behind tropical foliage.*

Anse Chastanet

*V*acationers wishing to put as little as possible between themselves and the Caribbean love Anse Chastanet, where the barrier between guests and the great outdoors can be just three exterior walls.

Soufrière, St. Lucia

(800) 223-1108

$$ – $$$$

beach

This hillside resort, the vision of architect and owner Nick Troubetzkoy, rises from a tranquil bay with its palm-lined beach to offer views of St. Lucia's spectacular twin Pitons. Troubetzkoy designed this singular resort to scale the hillside. The accommodations have unique features such as open-air showers, trees that sprout right up through guest rooms, and open walls — the view uninterrupted by windows or screens.

Oversized rooms, decorated West Indian style, range from beachside (most popular with divers) to hillside. The hillside rooms are the original accommodations, with screens and louvered windows. The trademark Troubetzkoy style is evident high up the hillside, where rooms have only three exterior walls and nature has been incorporated into the design. Rooms in block 7 have the best view of the Pitons and feature one-of-a-kind showers. The open-air shower in room 14B features a tree, while the shower in room 7F has a mirror that reflects the Pitons in the distance. Guest rooms have no telephones — vacationers check a board for messages near an outdoor bank of phones.

The resort atmosphere is pure St. Lucian. The Troubetzkoys are committed to preserving the island's natural and cultural resources, using locally made furnishings, fabrics, and artwork.

And food. Three restaurants offer a taste of local cuisine. Trou au Diable on the beachfront serves lunch daily as well as a Creole buffet dinner twice weekly. The Treehouse features fine dining: Creole and Continental entrées accompanied by wines from an extensive list. The Piton Restaurant offers breakfast — along with superb mountain views.

Recreation focuses on watersports, but the owners describe Anse Chastanet guests as "the kind of travelers who can entertain themselves."

ABOVE: Guests relax beneath thatched palapas at water's edge.

AT A GLANCE: *43 rooms and 6 suites, all with private balcony / patio, scenic view. 3 restaurants, spa, beauty salon, shops, tennis, hiking, nature walking, beach, scuba diving, snorkeling, windsurfing.*

Coconut-Stuffed Chicken Breast with Tomato Coulis

Tomato Coulis (yields 3 cups):
1 onion, finely chopped
2 garlic cloves, crushed
1 pound tomatoes, peeled, seeded,
　and finely chopped
1 cup chicken stock
1 small bunch of basil, finely chopped
Salt and pepper to taste

Coconut-Stuffed Chicken Breast:
4 boneless, skinless chicken breasts
Salt and pepper to taste
4 tablespoons butter, plus a few drops
　melted
1 medium onion, finely sliced
1 medium carrot, finely julienned
1 red bell pepper, seeded and finely
　julienned
1 green bell pepper, seeded and finely
　julienned
½ pound chayote (see note), finely
　julienned
1 celery stalk
2 cups freshly grated coconut, or
　2 cups shredded, unsweetened
1 cup fresh bread crumbs
1 egg, beaten

Prepare the coulis. Sauté the onion and garlic over low heat. Add the tomato and the chicken stock and simmer for 20 minutes, then process in a blender or food processor. Add the basil, reserving some for the garnish. Season.

Prepare the chicken. Preheat the oven to 350°F. Butter four pieces of aluminum foil, about 4 inches square.

Gently flatten the chicken breasts with a meat cleaver. Season and refrigerate.

Over medium heat, using 2 tablespoons of the butter, sauté the onion, carrot, bell pepper, chayote, and celery (the vegetables should remain crunchy). Allow to cool, then season.

Prepare the coconut crust. Mix the coconut and bread crumbs. Mix in the few drops of melted butter and half the beaten egg.

Place the breasts on the pieces of foil and fill the centers with the vegetable julienne. Roll the chicken tightly in the foil and bake for 8 minutes. Unwrap and brush with the rest of the beaten egg. Place a ¼-inch thickness of the coconut around each breast to form a crust. Sprinkle with the remaining butter and bake for another 8 minutes or until the coconut is golden brown.

To serve, pour the coulis in the center of each plate. Place the chicken on top, garnished with the reserved basil.

Note: Chayote, known as christophine or christophene in many French-speaking regions, is a pear-shaped squash available year round in selected supermarkets.

Yield: 4 servings

BELOW: *Trou au Diable offers a beachfront lunch on St. Lucia's salt-and pepper sands.*

Coco Reef Resort

> **O**nce the domain of scuba divers and nature lovers, Tobago is now also home to luxury hotels. Coco Reef Resort, the largest, is a destination for those seeking all the amenities of a sophisticated resort.

Tobago, Trinidad and Tobago

(800) 221-1294

$ – $$

beach

From an entrance highlighted by a Classic Rolls Royce Silver Cloud parked beneath a columned porte-cochere, to a breezy, open-air public area filled with wicker furniture, the tone here reflects that special Caribbean brand of elegance. The hotel management requests that guests not wear jeans, shorts, or T-shirts in public areas after seven in the evening.

The unique atmosphere is evident in Coco Reef's restaurants. Tamara's, an open-air dining room featuring international cuisine, also serves a buffet breakfast. Bacchanals, a casual beachside establishment, provides lunch and dinner in high season. The Gallery, an open-air bar that specializes in tropical concoctions, is the ideal spot to enjoy a wonderful Tobago sunset. Later, guests like to gather at Bobsters, an indoor bar that features murals depicting Caribbean musicians.

Coco Reef is located between two of the finest beaches in Tobago, but the hotel itself is situated on a man-made beach. Here calm waters, protected by a breakwater, provide an excellent playground for young swimmers. Snorkeling, windsurfing, and Sunfish sailing are available nearby.

A complete spa facility offers seaweed wraps, massage, facials, and Coco Reef's specialty, a mango rub body treatment.

Above: *Coco Reef Resort nestles its guests in the lap of luxury.*

At a glance: *96 rooms, 38 suites, 1 villa, all with private balcony/patio, ocean view. 2 restaurants, fitness center, spa, shops, outdoor pool, day/night tennis, bicycling, beach, snorkeling, windsurfing. Nearby: golf, hiking, nature walking, horseback riding, scuba diving, fishing.*

Marinated Duck Legs with Deep-Fried Vegetable Batons

Marinade:
2 cups white vinegar
1 cup soy sauce
½ cup honey
1½ garlic cloves, coarsely chopped
½ tablespoon ground coriander
Handful of black peppercorns

Duck:
12 pounds duck legs

Sauce:
8 cups duck or chicken stock

Vegetable Batons:
1 pound firm vegetables (such as carrots and squash), peeled and cut into 2 x ¼-inch batons
4 eggs
2 cups beer
1¾ cups all-purpose flour
¼ cup cornstarch
½ tablespoon baking powder
1 tablespoon saffron powder
Salt and pepper
1 cup water or milk

Prepare the marinade. Beat all the ingredients until smooth.

Prepare the duck. Marinate in the refrigerator for at least 24 hours, then transfer to a roasting pan. (Place the marinade in the freezer.) Bake the duck in a preheated 275°F oven for 2 hours, basting with its own juices every 30 minutes.

Prepare the sauce. Remove the marinade from the freezer and lift off the fat. Add one quarter of the mixture to the 8 cups of duck stock and, on the top of the stove, reduce to one quarter of the volume.

Prepare the vegetable batons. Blanch the vegetables for 5 minutes. Combine the rest of the ingredients to make a batter. If the batter is opaque, thin it out with water or milk. Dip the batons in the batter and deep fry.

To serve, place the vegetable batons in the center of each plate and arrange the duck legs on top. Pour the sauce on the plate, around the vegetables.

Yield: 8 – 10 servings

ABOVE: *Steel pan music keeps the atmosphere lively throughout Tobago.*

Grace Bay Club

L ocated on a stretch of the 12-mile beach at Grace Bay, this posh resort looks out over some of the most beautiful waters in the Caribbean.

Providenciales, Turks and Caicos

(800) 946-5757

$$$$

beach

Dazzling water laps at the shore just steps from the doors of the Grace Bay Club, and — best of all — it is water shared with very few other vacationers.

Here on the island of Providenciales, or just Provo to those guests fortunate enough to return again and again, it's always summertime, and the living is always easy.

Provo's most exclusive property is this Swiss-owned hotel, which values privacy first and foremost. The rooms, furnished with items from Mexico and India, are decorated in subdued beige tones to emphasize the brilliant color of the sea just beyond. Outside, Grace Bay Club's Spanish-style buildings, with their terracotta tiled roofs and stone columns, contrast with the deep blue of the Caribbean and the vivid hues of the hibiscus and bougainvillea.

At this resort the accent is on watersports, from Sunfish sailing to snorkeling in the pristine waters. Scuba diving, bonefishing, sea kayaking, and sailing excursions can be arranged.

Dining takes place at Anacaona, a Lucaya Indian word that means "flower of gold." This is also an accurate description of the cuisine, a Euro-Caribbean blend that favors fresh fruits and seafood from the island's bountiful waters — accompanied by wines from Anacaona's bountiful cellars. Chef Eric Brunel creates palate-pleasing dishes with a European base and a distinctive Caribbean flair. The meal is taken outdoors beneath thatched-roof palapas, the gentle sounds of the sea serving as background music. In the evening the ambiance is enhanced by the flickering lights of candles and tiki torches.

ABOVE: *The rooms are decorated with furnishings from around the world.*

AT A GLANCE: *21 suites with ocean view, some with private balcony / patio. Restaurant, whirlpool, beauty salon, shops, outdoor pool, day / night tennis, bicycling, beach, scuba diving, snorkeling, windsurfing, boating, fishing. NEARBY: fitness center, golf, hiking, nature walking, horseback riding, marina.*

Carpaccio of Tuna with Balsamic-Shallot Dressing

Balsamic-Shallot Dressing:
2 medium shallots, finely chopped
½ cup olive oil
¼ cup balsamic vinegar

Tuna:
6 ounces yellowfin tuna fillet, trimmed

Assembly:
4 ounces mixed lettuce leaves
Salt and pepper to taste
1 small bunch of chives, finely snipped

Prepare the dressing at least 60 minutes before serving time. Mix the shallot, oil, and vinegar.

Prepare the tuna. Cover with plastic wrap and place in the freezer for 60 minutes or until firm; do not freeze or it will become mushy. Then, using a kitchen slicing machine or a very sharp, thin-bladed knife, slice wafer-thin.

To serve, arrange the tuna slices around the entire inner rim of each plate. Drizzle a thin layer of the dressing over the tuna and refrigerate for 10 minutes. Toss the lettuce leaves with more dressing as well as salt and pepper and arrange around the tuna. Sprinkle with the chives.

Yield: 4 appetizer servings

. . . .
BELOW: *White powdery sand lies at the doorstep of the Grace Bay Club.*

Ocean Club

A sk members of the Ocean Club management to name the most popular activity at their resort and you'll get a refreshingly candid answer: Doing nothing at all.

And why not? Folks don't come to the remote Turks and Caicos for duty-free shopping, glitzy nightlife, or sightseeing tours. They come for the beach, the sun, and the clear-as-white rum waters of these tranquil islands.

Ocean Club, located on the island of Providenciales, began as a simple time-share but has blossomed to full resort status, with a restaurant, beach grill, two bars, small shopping arcade, and watersports concession. Expansive public areas, vast, richly landscaped grounds, and a sprawling beachfront keep it uncrowded and peaceful. Many guests choose to dine in their suites (which feature kitchen or kitchenette, as well as washer/dryer) and start their mornings with a walk in robe and slippers to the beachfront grill for a cup of coffee and a croissant to take back to their screened patio.

To help start their engines, or to help them wind down after a day of "doing nothing at all," guests can amble over to the fitness center for massages and aromatherapy.

The white sandy beach just steps from the suites is one of the chief assets of this resort. Water lovers can also choose from two freshwater pools, including a freeform pool that's popular with children. Art Pickering's Provo Turtle Divers, located at the resort, offers dive excursions, snorkel trips, bonefishing and deep-sea fishing, parasailing, and scuba certification. Resort courses in the Ocean Club pool provide an orientation to scuba. A shallow reef dive offshore follows.

A day of sun and surf builds a healthy appetite. The Ocean Club Cabana Bar and Grille serves snacks and drinks throughout the day as well as breakfast and lunch. The breakfast honor system exemplifies the relaxed atmosphere at this resort: guests check off buffet items on their ticket and sign out the meals to their room. The Gecko Grill features both indoor and al fresco dining with an international menu: soups and salads, pastas, brick-oven pizzas, and grilled dishes such as Provo grouper and Caribbean lobster. A children's menu is available.

ABOVE: Cool trade winds for everyone: each room features a screened porch.

AT A GLANCE: *86 suites with private balcony, ocean/island view. 2 restaurants, fitness center, shops, outdoor pool, day/night tennis, bicycling, hiking, nature walking, beach, scuba diving, snorkeling, windsurfing, boating, fishing.* NEARBY: *golf, marina, casino.*

Grouper Macadamia with Pineapple-Tomato Salsa

Pineapple-Tomato Salsa (yields 5½ cups):

2 cups finely diced pineapple

10 plum tomatoes, peeled, seeded, and diced

¼ cup diced green bell pepper

¼ cup thinly sliced scallions

¼ cup diced onion

6 garlic cloves, chopped

1 or 2 jalapeños, seeded and finely chopped

1 bunch of cilantro, chopped

¼ cup white vinegar

½ cup olive oil

1 tablespoon salt

1 tablespoon black pepper

Fish:

2 pounds grouper fillets, cut into 4-ounce portions

2 tablespoons butter

1 tablespoon salt

1 tablespoon pepper

Juice of 1 lime

1 avocado, pitted, peeled, and puréed

½ cup macadamia nuts, toasted and coarsely chopped

Garnish:

4 lemon wedges

4 lime wedges

8 sprigs of cilantro

Prepare the salsa. Combine all the ingredients in a bowl and mix until blended. Adjust the seasoning. Refrigerate.

Prepare the fish. Preheat the oven to 350°F. Place the grouper in a baking pan greased with the butter. Season with the salt and pepper and bake for 5 – 10 minutes or until nearly done. Add the lime juice to the avocado purée and spread this on top of the fish. Sprinkle with the nuts. Return to the oven until the nuts are hot and the fish flakes easily with a fork.

To serve, place a dollop of the salsa in the center of each plate. Arrange 1 piece of fish on each side. Garnish with the lemon and lime wedges topped with 2 of the cilantro sprigs.

Yield: 4 servings

. . . .

BELOW: *Spacious grounds and a sprawling beachfront: the Ocean Club is a true tropical paradise.*

Buccaneer Resort

*C*aribbean resorts that focus on family activities are in no short supply — the Islands feature many spots where sandcastle-building takes priority over disco dancing and gambling.

St. Croix, USVI

(800) 255-3881

$$$

beach / golf / tennis

But, even in the Caribbean, you'd be hard-pressed to find another resort like St. Croix's Buccaneer Resort, where the family is actually behind the desk — not to mention in the gift shops, on the golf courses, and out on the bougainvillea-dotted grounds chatting with guests.

Nine generations of the Armstrong family have called St. Croix home. Since the early 1920s, this family has owned an estate on the north side of the island. In 1653, the rambling property belonged to Charles Martel, a Knight of Malta, who built the manor as a veritable fortress, with walls three feet thick. Tucked behind a hill, out of sight of marauding pirates, the stately home was later the residence of the young Alexander Hamilton. A century later it was a sugar plantation.

In 1948, the manor was remodeled, its fortress walls forming the perimeter of a swimming pool, and divided into 11 guest rooms. Douglas and Rachel Armstrong and their family were ready to welcome the harbingers of St. Croix's bustling tourist trade.

Today's guests stay in the three-hundred-year-old manor itself or in beachside villas that hug the palm-shaded shoreline. Tennis and golf occupy the days of landlubbers. Water enthusiasts take half-day and full-day snorkel trips to nearby Buck Island, site of an underwater nature trail.

Diners have several restaurants from which to choose. The Terrace, an open-air establishment boasting one of the finest views in the Virgin Islands, serves breakfast and dinner. The Mermaid, adjacent to the beach, serves lunch, featuring local specialties like fungi and conch as well as light choices such as fruit salad. For a special evening, Dino's, overlooking the lights of Christiansted, serves Italian and Mediterranean favorites in elegant surroundings.

ABOVE: Once the estate of a Knight of Malta, this has been a family-run resort for half a century.

AT A GLANCE: *132 rooms with private balcony / patio, ocean / mountain view; 5 suites with Jacuzzi. 4 restaurants, fitness center, spa, sauna, beauty salon, shops, movie theaters, supervised children's programs, outdoor pool, day / night tennis, golf, hiking, nature walking, beach, scuba diving, snorkeling, windsurfing, boating.* NEARBY: *bicycling, horseback riding, fishing.*

Potage Cornell
(Pumpkin and Sweet Potato Soup)

This soup is named for the Buccaneer Resort's Antiguan-born sous chef, Deryck Cornell Henry, who contributed his extensive knowledge of seasonings and local ingredients to its creation.

3 pounds Caribbean pumpkin, peeled, seeded, and cut into 1- or 2-inch cubes (ordinary pumpkin can be substituted)

1½ pounds white sweet potatoes, peeled and cut into 1-inch cubes (see note)

1½ pounds Spanish onions, diced medium

4 tablespoons chopped garlic

2 – 3 tablespoons olive oil

1 (14-ounce) can of Thai milk or unsweetened coconut milk

1 tablespoon Thai red curry paste or Jamaican curry powder

1½ tablespoons minced herbs (such as parsley, thyme, and rosemary)

Salt and white pepper to taste

Boil the pumpkin and sweet potato until soft. Put through a sieve, reserving the liquid.

Sauté the onion and garlic in the oil until caramelized.

Purée the pumpkin mixture together with the onion and garlic. In a heavy pot, bring the purée to a simmer over medium heat. Add the Thai milk and curry paste and simmer for 5 minutes. Add the herbs. Season with the salt and pepper. Adjust the consistency, if desired, with the reserved pumpkin-potato liquid.

Note: The white sweet potato is, in fact, not sweet. When cooked, it is similar in taste and texture to the baking potato. One pound of orange-fleshed sweet potatoes and a half pound of baking potatoes can be substituted.

Yield: 10 servings

· · · · · · · · ·

ABOVE: *Beautiful beaches delight guests of the Buccaneer Resort.*

Renaissance Grand Beach Resort

*Y*ou can't keep a good resort down. Struck by Hurricane Marilyn in 1995, the aptly named Renaissance Grand Beach Resort rose like a phoenix from the ashes to re-open even grander than before.

St. Thomas, USVI

(800) HOTELS-1

$$

beach

From the moment guests step into the open-air lobby and see the pristine beach and the Caribbean Sea beyond, they love the tropical décor and cool, airy feel of this resort.

Activity centers on the sea. Guests can simply step out onto the beach, pull up a chaise longue, and have a lazy day in the sun. For those who'd rather pursue fun in the water, the Renaissance Grand Beach features snorkeling, sailing, kayaking, and windsurfing.

The resort is an excellent base from which to tour the Island. St. Thomas's poinciana-covered hills overlook streets that offer some of the Caribbean's finest duty-free shopping. The busy, cosmopolitan town of Charlotte Amalie (pronounced a-mal-yah) has the makings of a full day of shopping opportunities in waterfront shops, many of them located in centuries-old Danish warehouses.

Another popular day-trip destination is the neighboring U.S. Virgin Island of St. John, two thirds of which is preserved as a national park. It's just a 20-minute ferry ride from the community of Red Hook, near the Renaissance Grand Beach Resort, to this charming island.

Rooms at the Renaissance Grand Beach, which is constructed on one of St. Thomas's steep hillsides, look out onto the palm-shaded beach and the turquoise sea.

The resort has two specialty restaurants and also serves poolside lunches (don't miss the resident iguana begging for French fries!). The dining highlight of the week is Sunday brunch, featuring local seafood and other island specialties as well as a 12-foot Bloody Mary bar.

ABOVE: Rooms at the Renaissance Grand Beach Resort overlook a marvelous beach.

AT A GLANCE: *254 rooms with private balcony/patio, sea/island view; 36 suites with Jacuzzi, private balcony/patio, sea/island view. 2 restaurants, fitness center, steam room, sauna, beauty salon, shops, supervised children's programs, outdoor pool, day/night tennis, nature walking, jogging, beach, scuba diving, snorkeling, windsurfing, boating, fishing, sailing excursions. NEARBY: golf.*

Tropical Chicken Breast

To evoke the warm tropical breezes of the Caribbean, do as the Renaissance Grand Beach Resort does and serve each chicken breast in half a scooped-out coconut shell.

6 boneless, skinless chicken breasts
1½ teaspoons salt
¼ teaspoon pepper
½ teaspoon paprika
½ cup all-purpose flour
8 tablespoons butter
1 honeydew melon, scooped into balls
1 cantaloupe, scooped into balls
1 papaya, scooped into balls
¼ cup sherry
1 cup coconut milk
1 cup brown sauce
½ cup whipping cream
¼ cup unsweetened shredded
   coconut, toasted

Season the chicken with the salt, pepper, and paprika. Sprinkle with the flour and sauté on both sides in 6 tablespoons of the butter until lightly browned.

Add the melon, cantaloupe, and papaya balls (reserving some for the garnish), sherry, and coconut milk. Simmer for 5 minutes, then remove the fruit. Add the brown sauce and the cream and simmer until the chicken is tender.

Remove the chicken and reduce the sauce until thick and of serving consistency. Stir in the remaining 2 tablespoons of butter. Season to taste.

Place a chicken breast on each plate (or on a coconut half shell). Cover with the sauce and serve garnished with the reserved melon, cantaloupe, and papaya balls and the shredded coconut.

Yield: 6 servings

· · · · · · · · ·

BELOW: *St. Thomas's Charlotte Amalie, one of the Caribbean's most beautiful ports, offers unrivaled duty-free shopping.*

Acapulco Princess

T**he Acapulco Princess is a miniature city on Acapulco's southern shore. Tucked away behind a veritable forest of palm trees, this deluxe hideaway is the kind of place that vacationers enter and never leave until it's time to go home.**

Acapulco, Mexico

(800) 223-1818

$$$

beach

And there's no *reason* to leave this resort. Golf, tennis, watersports, tropical flowers, gourmet dining — you name it — are all to be found at this magnificent one-stop vacation spot.

The grounds of the Acapulco Princess, featuring 750 varieties of plant life as well as swans, peacocks, and flamingoes, are the first thing to catch the eye. The 480-acre resort is a virtual botanical garden. The architecture of the Acapulco Princess is the next thing to catch the eye: this is not your standard high-rise hotel, but an Aztec temple set in a jungle of tropical growth, where waterfalls spill out into freeform pools and the laughter of guests is echoed in the calls of exotic birds.

Dining here is an international experience. French cuisine is served at Le Gourmet restaurant, while classic Mexican specialties and steaks are the order of the day at La Hacienda. Two other restaurants feature al fresco buffet dining. And if a day of golf and watersports still leaves guests uneasy about their calorie count, they can dance the night away at the pulsating Club Pyramid. This disco, which features pre-Columbian décor and high-tech special effects, throbs with the spirit of Acapulco.

Guests at the Acapulco Princess are entitled to use the facilities of the 344-room Pierre Marques, a seasonal sister hotel adjacent to the resort. Built by J. Paul Getty as a personal hideaway, it is today a quiet retreat with a country club atmosphere. Shuttle between these two resorts is complimentary for guests.

ABOVE: *This hotel resembles an Aztec temple.*

AT A GLANCE: *914 rooms and 105 suites, all with private balcony, grounds / golf course view. 5 restaurants (seasonal), fitness center, spa, beauty salon, shops, outdoor pools, indoor / outdoor / night tennis, golf, beach.* NEARBY: *movie theaters, horseback riding, scuba diving, snorkeling, windsurfing, boating, fishing.*

Guacamole

3 medium avocados, pitted and peeled
1 small onion, finely diced
1 medium tomato, unpeeled, finely
   diced
2 garlic cloves, finely minced
3 green chilies, seeded and minced
1 teaspoon lemon juice
5 sprigs of cilantro, coarsely chopped
Salt and white pepper to taste
Tortilla chips

Mash the avocados to a pulpy, coarse consistency and place in a china or stainless steel bowl.

Add the other ingredients and mix well but quickly with a fork or wooden spoon. Mix only once. The consistency should be creamy, coarse, and somewhat dry.

Serve at room temperature, with tortilla chips.

Yield: 2 cups

BELOW: *The sounds of waterfalls and tropical birds blend with mariachi music at the Acapulco Princess.*

Fiesta Americana Condesa Acapulco

A capulco. It's glitzy. It's glamorous. It's Hollywood with a fiesta spirit. This beautiful port city, filled with the vacation homes of some of the silver screen's biggest names, is a favorite haunt of the rich and famous.

Acapulco, Mexico

(800) FIESTA 1

$

beach

But it's not just the jet-setters who get to enjoy Acapulco's magnificent beaches and spirited nightlife. The Fiesta Americana Condesa Acapulco appeals to the average person or family seeking good prices (children under 12 sharing a parent's room are not charged for accommodation or meals). Location is another draw, with the resort's view of spectacular Acapulco Bay, proximity to shops, and promise of round-the-clock fun.

Days at the Fiesta Americana can be as busy or as blissful as you choose. You can stroll the Costera and shop at fashionable boutiques for designer clothing or at charming mercados for local crafts. You can don a mask and snorkel in the crystal-clear waters off the Fiesta Americana beach, or take an excursion to La Quebrada to watch the cliff divers make their death-defying leaps. Or you can just sip a margarita while floating weightlessly in the pool. However you decide to spend your day, it's always a thrill to watch the sun set over the bay and see the lights come on to greet another pulsating Acapulco night.

Dining options include La Trattoria, for Italian cuisine in an elegant setting, and the poolside Chula Vista restaurant. For many guests, the perfect midday break is lunch at one of three poolside snack bars that feature local favorites, often to the beat of live music.

ABOVE: Guests of this resort can choose between a beautiful pool and a wide swath of sand.

AT A GLANCE: *487 rooms and 13 suites, all with private balcony, ocean / Acapulco view. 4 restaurants, fitness center, beauty salon, shops, supervised children's programs, outdoor pool, tennis, beach, watersports, scuba diving, fishing.* NEARBY: *movie theaters, golf, boating.*

Black Bean Soup

2 (15-ounce) cans cooked black beans,
  drained
10 strips bacon, diced ¼ inch
¼ cup butter
6 garlic cloves, minced
½ white onion, diced
Black pepper to taste
Powdered chicken stock to taste
5 cups tortilla chips
4 cups grated Cheddar cheese
1 cup sour cream
2½ avocados, pitted, peeled, and sliced
1 cup of cilantro sprigs, chopped

Purée the beans in a food processor, adding water to achieve a desirable consistency.

Sauté the bacon, butter, garlic, onion, and bean purée. Season with the pepper and chicken stock.

Serve in bowls, garnished with the tortilla chips, cheese, sour cream, a slice of avocado, and cilantro.

Yield: 10 servings

· · · · · · · · · ·

BELOW: *With its view of Acapulco Bay and its proximity to shops, the Fiesta Americana Condesa Acapulco pleases every type of guest.*

Fiesta Americana Coral Beach Cancún

Cancún. Water as clear as tequila. History as ancient as the Mayan civilization. Atmosphere as hot as the temperature. These features combine to make this city — and this resort — a top vacation spot.

Cancún, Mexico

(800) FIESTA 1

$$

beach

Like most of Cancún's fine hotels, the Fiesta Americana Coral Beach Cancún is located in the Hotel Zone on Kukulcan Boulevard, the fashionable strip that stretches for 12 miles, the entire length of Cancún Island. The strip is lined with deluxe high-rise resorts that dazzle their guests with plush rooms, gourmet restaurants, and lively discos.

The Fiesta Americana is one of the most luxurious on the island and one of only two hotels in Mexico to earn the AAA Five Diamond rating. This sprawling hotel features a spacious layout. Its huge, opulent lobby is decorated in imported marble, illuminated through a stained-glass ceiling, and filled with palm trees.

Days center around the chalk-white beaches and the hotel's six-hundred-square-foot multi-level swimming pool, complete with waterfall.

Evenings are for dressing up and dining in one of this resort's four outstanding restaurants: La Joya for haute cuisine, the Vina del Mar Café for international specialties with an ocean view, the Coral Reef for gourmet seafood, and the Isla Contoy for al fresco dining.

ABOVE: *Of all the deluxe hotels that line Kukulcan Boulevard, this is perhaps the most spectacular.*

AT A GLANCE: *602 suites with private balcony, some with Jacuzzi, ocean view. 4 restaurants, fitness center, spa, steam room, beauty salon, shops, supervised children's programs, outdoor pool, indoor tennis, beach, watersports.* NEARBY: *movie theaters, golf, bicycling, rollerblading, horseback riding, scuba diving, snorkeling, boating, fishing.*

Tenderloin Medallions La Joya

Sauce:

½ ounce mixed dried chilies (such
    as guajillo, pasilla, and ancho)
    (see note 1)

1 white onion, sliced

5 garlic cloves

½ pound tomatoes

Chopped thyme to taste

1 bay leaf

Ground cumin to taste

Salt and pepper to taste

Tenderloin Medallions:

1 pound cactus leaves (see note 2)

8 beef tenderloin medallions

Salt and pepper to taste

4 scallions

4 dried chilies

2 plantains, each cut lengthwise into
    4 (¼-inch) slices

¼ cup corn oil

4 sprigs of cilantro

Sesame seeds

Prepare the sauce. Boil all the ingredients until the chilies are tender. Purée in a blender or food processor, then bring to a boil and simmer until the consistency is neither watery nor too thick. Adjust the seasoning with salt and pepper and strain through a fine sieve. Keep warm.

Prepare the tenderloin medallions. Using a cookie cutter, cut the cactus leaves into 8 (1½-inch) rounds, reserving one leaf to cut into 12 (1-inch) diamonds for the garnish.

Grill the beef, seasoned with the salt and pepper. Grill the scallions, chilies, and cactus rounds. Fry the plantain in the oil.

To serve, place 3 cactus diamonds and 2 plantain slices on one side of each plate. Place 2 cactus rounds on the other side and top each round with a medallion. Cover the medallions with the sauce. Place a grilled chili and a grilled scallion between the medallions. Add a sprig of cilantro and sprinkle with the sesame seeds.

Note 1: The smooth, burnished red guajillo, which measures 4 inches by 1 inch, is hot and very tough. It must be soaked longer than most dried chilies. The dark-brown pasilla, called a chilaca in its fresh form, is 6 – 8 inches long and medium hot. For a description of the ancho chili, see note 1 on page 49.

Note 2: The fleshy oval leaves, called pads or paddles, of the nopal (prickly pear) cactus are available year round in Mexican markets and some supermarkets. These have a taste similar to green beans.

Yield: 4 servings

BELOW: *The Fiesta Americana Coral Beach Cancún has a multi-level swimming pool.*

Marriott CasaMagna Cancún

*L*uxury hotels tower above the palms. Fine restaurants offer cuisine from around the world. Shops tempt travelers with trinkets ranging from Colombian emeralds to French perfumes to Italian leathers.

Cancún, Mexico

(800) 223-6388

$ – $$

beach

Selected as the ideal resort location by a computer two and a half decades ago, Cancún is now a five-star tourist city. The lavishness is evident at resorts like the Marriott CasaMagna Cancún, which is located in the Hotel Zone. Set on a wide swath of powdery white sand, this deluxe resort is designed to resemble a Roman palace. White columns lead up to guest-room balconies from which tropical plants cascade. In the center of the U-shaped complex, an enormous swimming pool competes for attention with the clear waters of the Caribbean.

For all its splendor, however, this is a family resort. Children are welcome at the Marriott CasaMagna Cancún. The family package entitles them to membership in Club Amigos, while everyone receives a pass for the new Wet 'n Wild Water Park, featuring dolphins, a wave pool, and water slides. Every member of the family will enjoy excursions to nearby attractions such as the Mayan ruins, the Sian Ka'an Biosphere Reserve, and Xcaret, where visitors can swim in an underground river.

After a day in the sun, the evening proves equally sizzling. Dining choices range from American and Mexican specialties at La Capilla to a Japanese steakhouse that serves meals at Teppan Yaki-style tables. Hotel guests can continue their revelry at an oceanside bar or in the lobby lounge.

ABOVE: *Roman columns lead to the balconies of guest rooms at this palatial resort.*

AT A GLANCE: *450 rooms with Jacuzzi, private balcony, ocean/lagoon view; 38 suites with whirlpool, private balcony, ocean/lagoon view, 1 with whirlpool, Jacuzzi. 4 restaurants, fitness center, spa, sauna, whirlpool, beauty salon, shops, supervised children's programs, outdoor pool, day/night tennis, beach, watersports.* NEARBY: *golf, scuba diving, snorkeling, windsurfing, boating, fishing.*

Margarita Pie

This recipe from La Capilla restaurant at the Marriott CasaMagna Cancún is often requested by guests. Executive chef Ross Randall estimates that he makes 30 margarita pies every week.

Crust:

8 ounces pretzels, salted or unsalted
½ cup sugar
9 ounces butter, melted

Filling:

¾ cup lime juice
½ tablespoon plain gelatin
4 eggs, separated
1¼ cups sugar
1 tablespoon grated lime rind
½ cup tequila
¼ cup orange-flavored liqueur

Prepare the crust. Lightly grease a 10-inch springform pan. Crush the pretzels to a medium fineness. Add the sugar, then the butter. Turn the mixture into the pan and press lightly so that all surfaces are covered. Refrigerate.

Prepare the filling. Sprinkle the lime juice over the gelatin and let stand until the gelatin softens.

Beat the egg yolks in the top of a double boiler. Blend in half the sugar and the rind. Add the softened gelatin and cook over boiling water, stirring constantly, until the mixture is slightly thickened and the gelatin is completely dissolved. Transfer to a chilled bowl. Blend in the tequila and the liqueur and refrigerate until cold but not thickened.

Beat the egg whites until foamy. Gradually beat in the remaining sugar until soft peaks form. Carefully fold the cooled egg-yolk mixture into the beaten egg whites a third at a time, ensuring that the two mixtures are completely combined before making each new addition.

Set the bowl over ice and let stand, stirring frequently, until the mixture mounds on a spoon. Swirl it into the chilled crust.

Refrigerate for 2 hours before serving.
Yield: 1 (10-inch) pie

. . . .
ABOVE: *Margarita pie is a hit with diners at Marriott Casa-Magna Cancún's La Capilla restaurant.*

Index

Resorts

Metric Equivalents

General Formula for Metric Conversion

Ounces to grams: multiply ounce figure by 28.35.

Pounds to grams: multiply pound figure by 453.59.

Pounds to kilograms: multiply pound figure by 0.45.

Ounces to milliliters: multiply ounce figure by 30.

Cups to liters: multiply cup figure by 0.24.

Fahrenheit to Celsius: subtract 32 from the Fahrenheit figure, multiply by 5, then divide by 9.

Inches to centimeters: multiply inch figure by 2.54.

Volume

1 ounce = 28 grams
1 pound = 454 grams

Weight

1 teaspoon = 5 milliliters
1 tablespoon = 15 milliliters
¼ cup = 60 milliliters
⅓ cup = 80 milliliters
½ cup = 120 milliliters
⅔ cup = 160 milliliters
1 cup = 230 milliliters

Oven Temperatures

300°F = 150°C
325°F = 165°C
350°F = 175°C
375°F = 190°C
400°F = 200°C
425°F = 220°C
450°F = 230°C
475°F = 245°C